The Power of
MANTRA &
The Mystery of
INITIATION

Also by Pandit Rajmani Tigunait

Tantra Unveiled

Swami Rama of the Himalayas: His Life and Mission

Shakti: The Power in Tantra (A Scholarly Approach)

From Death to Birth: Understanding Karma and Reincarnation

Inner Quest

Shakti Sadhana: Steps to Samadhi
(A Translation of the Tripura Rahasya)

The Tradition of the Himalayan Masters

Yoga on War and Peace

Seven Systems of Indian Philosophy

Videos

In the Footsteps of the Sages

Living Tantra™ Seminar Series

 Tantric Traditions and Techniques

 The Secret of Tantric Rituals

 Forbidden Tantra

 Tantra and Kundalini

 Sri Chakra: The Highest Tantric Practice

 Sri Vidya: The Embodiment of Tantra

Audio

Eight Steps to Self-Transformation

Nine Steps to Disarming the Mind

The Power of

MANTRA &

The Mystery of

INITIATION

BY
PANDIT RAJMANI TIGUNAIT, PH.D.

Himalayan Institute Press
Honesdale, Pennsylvania

Dedicated to my gurudeva,

Sri Swami Rama of the Himalayas,
the one who uttered His name and
kindly accepted my little "I" and
offered it at the feet of Mother Divine.

CONTENTS

Man shall not live by bread alone,

but by every word that proceedeth

out of the mouth of God.

Matthew 4:4

INTRODUCTION

This book was first conceived as a spiritual diary, a mirror in which to see the reflection of my own mind and spiritual self. Initially it emerged in the form of a simple, but deep, contemplative thought as I saw fear, doubt, insecurity, and guilt in a student who visited me for mantra initiation in the fall of 1993.

This man had been coming to the Himalayan Institute, where I am a teacher, for several years. He took weekend courses on meditation, the science of breath, and hatha yoga, and finally he spent a month in residence. He asked for an appointment for mantra initiation only after a long debate with himself, as I found out later. So when the day came I initiated him into mantra meditation, following the instructions of my master. Afterwards, I invited him to come and see me if he had any questions after practicing the mantra. A few days later, he came and shared his experience with me. It was not a particularly uncommon experience, but somehow it released a flood of thought I had never experienced before.

The student reported that since receiving mantra initiation he had been experiencing a great sense of joy. His concentration was good, and as the sound of the mantra emerged in his mind his entire being was infused with peace. He realized that he had at last found the peace and tranquility he had been seeking for so long. But after a day or two, fear set in. He began thinking, "Is this a magical spell? It is too peaceful. Will I be able to enjoy life as I used to? How will I be able to relate to my friends, who live a wild life? This kind of joy might suck me into yoga completely. I want to be happy, but I do not want to lose my competitive edge in business or the kind of self I used to cherish."

During our conversation this gentleman shared something else with me: He was scared of my master and the sages of our lineage. During the initiation I had said, "On behalf of my master, Sri Swami Rama, and the sages of the lineage this mantra is given to you." This statement and the peace he experienced during and after the initiation led him to believe that Swamiji must be an unbelievably powerful person. His reasoning was that if Pandit Rajmani could do such things on his behalf, what would happen if Swamiji himself initiated someone?

In addition to harboring these doubts and fears, he was also feeling guilty because he was attempting to find God in a domain that was not part of his background. I attempted to console him by reminding him of what Christ says in the fourth chapter of Mark: "The sower soweth the word. . . . but when they have heard, Satan cometh immediately, and taketh away the word that was sown in their hearts."

"My friend," I continued, "You were looking for peace, tranquility of mind, and one-pointedness. Through the grace of God you got them. Try not to lose them. Your fears, doubts, insecurities, and guilt are baseless. The seed of the word is there. Let it grow and blossom.

"Try to analyze the source of your fear. Isn't it that you are afraid of being fearless, clear, one-pointed, and self-loving? Isn't it that you are afraid of doubting your doubt or confronting your own negativity? Ask yourself, 'What's wrong if I'm happy?'

"As far as your fear of spiritual teachers is concerned, please remember that a human being has no power. It is the might of the Almighty that manifests in the form of love, compassion, kindness, and knowledge in human hearts. These godly virtues can never have an adverse effect on us. No entity other than God has the power to exert any kind of influence on us—God alone is the power of all powers, the pool of primordial divine energy. To be fearful of anyone is to block the flow of divine radiance.

"Therefore, I advise you to continue doing your mantra lovingly, respectfully, and faithfully. Please don't let the Satan living in the unlit corner of your mind drag the idea of Sri Swamiji, other sages, or me into your spiritual crisis. Counsel the brighter part of your soul to emerge victorious in this inner battle. Let the soul, not the mind—which is inflicted with fear, doubt, insecurity, and guilt—decide whether or not you follow the path of meditation."

This gentlemen left a few days after our conversation. I do not know what path he chose, but this incident lingered in my mind. For some reason the feeling generated by this simple encounter continued to intensify. A tiny wave was turning into a tide, and the fact that Sri Swamiji was not in residence at the Institute was causing that tide to gain momentum.

It was at this time that Swamiji shifted his energy wholly to the Himalayan Institute Hospital, a charitable project in the foothills of the Himalayas. Never before in the twenty-five years he had worked in the West had he focused so one-pointedly on a project in India. This drastic change in his working style was a clear indication that he would be spending most of his time in India and very little in any other part of the world. This unspoken decision was apparently affecting the minds and hearts of a large number of students in a fashion similar to the way the gentleman who had come for initiation had been affected. I watched as a cloud of fear, doubt, anger, and insecurity began swirling around.

One day, as I was walking home from my office, I found myself totally absorbed in the world of my own thoughts. "Are the manifestations of these tendencies necessary stages in our spiritual quest? What brings us to this path, and what causes us to leave it? What motivates us to become great seekers for a while, yet why do most of us eventually turn against that which we so dearly sought?"

With these questions turning in my mind, I began re-reading scriptures I had read many times in the past: the *Ramayana,* the *Bhagavad Gita,* the *Yoga Vasishtha,* and the Upanishads. The questions I had been contemplating were so compelling that it seemed as I read that they were looking for answers on their own. And each time the answers manifested in the scriptures, I heard the affirming voices of Sri Swamiji and other great souls—Swami Krishnananda, Sadananda, and Chaitanya Prakashananda—who had in the past kindly and unconditionally guided me on the path.

I noticed that the answers to all my questions centered around two central themes. The first theme was to be careful of fear and doubt. Fear and doubt are like an army of termites chewing away at the foundation and causing the entire structure of spirituality to collapse. The second theme was that ego and selfishness are the greatest enemies. In fact they are the commanders—they organize anger, hatred, jealousy, greed, and the desire for revenge, commanding them to create both inner and outer turmoil.

Some people are disappointed and discouraged to find that the scriptures and the saints stress our negative qualities. At first it may seem that they had a pessimistic attitude toward spirituality, but as I thought about it I began to realize that this is not the case: the scriptures are neither pessimistic nor optimistic; they are neither negative nor positive—they are simply stating facts. If we know these facts, we can continue our journey without becoming discouraged.

A passage in the monumental work the *Ramayana,* by the medieval Indian saint Tulsidas, helped me to organize my thoughts and delve further into the subject of spirituality with an objective attitude. He said:

> Spirituality is like a lake of immortal nectar. It is impossible to reach this lake without the grace of God. Bad company distorts the path that leads there. Rumors spread by bad company are like tigers and cobras that inhabit the path. Worldliness and day-to-day domestic concerns are like impassable mountains. Ignorance, delusion, ego, and vanity are like a dense forest. Mental gibberish, which causes doubt and destructive reasoning, is like a tumultuous river one must cross in order to reach the lake that lies beyond. This lake of spirituality is unreachable for those who are not endowed with the

power of unshakable faith, for those who are not blessed with the company of wise people, and for those for whom God is not the dearest one.

If by chance [out of curiosity, because spirituality has become a fad, or because frustrated worldly ambitions create a sense of being fed up with the world] one happens to follow this path and endure its hardships, the trio of sloth, inertia, and complacency, led by ignorance, will cause sleep to descend just short of the shoreline. While lying inert, such a seeker blames the cool breeze for destroying the scorching heat of his worldliness and refuses to take a sip of the immortal nectar. Thus without attaining the goal, which he had almost achieved, he reverts to his old ways and boasts about his journey. When someone asks about the lake he replies, "I've been there and seen what it really is. Don't bother to go—it's not worth it."

However, a person blessed with the grace of God is not affected by any of these obstacles. Such a blessed one reaches the lake, sips the immortal nectar with reverence, and attains freedom from threefold pain: physical, mental, and spiritual. Under no circumstance does such an aspirant abandon this lake.

Therefore, because all obstacles begin with bad company, anyone who wants to sip from this lake must resort to *satsanga* [the company of saintly souls].

I was struck by the wisdom and profundity of this passage.

Yet I continued to wonder: In today's circumstances where do we seek and find the company of saintly souls? How do we know who is a saint and who is not? In the Western tradition a person is declared a saint long after he or she is dead, so to have that person's company is only an abstract idea.

In Eastern traditions a saint is defined in extremely broad terms—anybody can be called a saint, and there is no way of proving or disproving it. The external paraphernalia surrounding sainthood differs from tradition to tradition, and the internal qualities of sainthood (such as unconditional love, compassion, selflessness, and the direct experience of inner truth) are extremely subtle—and therefore—invisible.

Furthermore, in the hectic pace of the modern world, who has time to search for saints and enjoy their company? Just as in other areas of inquiry, therefore, we begin our search through books, audiotapes, videos, or courses. And through these sources we gather general information which inspires us to seek personal guidance. That's where the scary part of the journey begins. We must take a risk—there does not seem to be a way to embark on and complete the journey to impersonal universal Truth without receiving personal guidance from an experienced mentor.

The more I pondered the nature of personal guidance, the more I realized that in all times and places the name of God, or the sacred Word, has been the core of spirituality. Further, it is by receiving the Word directly from a teacher that a student establishes a connection with the path that leads directly to the highest goal. This understanding finally led me to explore the dynamics of the Divine Word—its relationship with the Absolute and the sage to whom it was originally revealed, the process through which the Word has been passed on from generation to generation, and how the Word purifies our minds and hearts.

To expand my own vision I explored scriptures from both yogic and non-yogic traditions. In my search I found that the sacred sound is universal, and that through untold ages and in cultures throughout the world the idea of the sacred Word has been a source of wonder, excitement, and mystery. Even now, in this technologically advanced era, people rely on the healing power of sacred sound, the transformative power of mantra, and the calming effect of spiritually awakened music.

Because an invisible protective force lies in sacred words, the yoga tradition calls such words *mantra*—literally, "the word which protects just by the virtue of being repeated" (*mananat trayate iti mantrah*). In India, thinkers, philosophers, scientists, and spiritual teachers have devoted vast amounts of time and energy to discovering the dynamics of the Divine Word, which according to the scriptures is the force from which life manifests in all its diversity. Texts documenting the discoveries related to the sacred sound are called mantra *shastra,* and this particular branch of learning is called mantra *vidya.*

Through the millennia the sages delved into the minute details of this science, discovering the precise application of specific sounds, not only for spiritual unfoldment but also for worldly success. Consequently mantra science pervaded such fields as medicine, astrology, numerology, dance, painting, and music. Its applications range from procuring a good harvest, attaining success in business, finding the right spouse, curing a snake bite, improving retentive power, and unfolding inner peace, all the way to attaining freedom from the cycle of birth and death. We read the texts of mantra *shastra* and the biographies of saints and yogis and are thrilled by the stories of the miraculous powers that accompany mantras. But very few of us witness such powers firsthand—and even if we do, we are puzzled by them.

So I set out to write this book to explain why mantras contain miraculous powers. Drawing from the scriptures and from the experiences of saints and yogis whom I have met in the course of my life, I offer an explanation in these pages of why in some cases mantras exhibit their powers, but hardly show any effect in others. This book also explains how, from the power of mantra, God, who is all-mighty, all-pervasive, and infinite, becomes finite enough to be seen by us—in other words, how the impersonal becomes personal. This work demonstrates that the relationship between mantra and Absolute Reality and the materialization of a personified form of God from the power of mantra is the ground on which various aspects of yoga, meditation, spirituality, and mysticism (such as kundalini, chakra, yantra, mandala, and Tantra) meet.

The last chapter focuses on the most esoteric or mystical aspect of this science: *shaktipata* (the direct transmission of spiritual energy). To help seekers overcome the confusion caused by sensational stories and propaganda about *shaktipata,* this book takes the reader to original sources—the scriptures on the subject and the experiences of the adepts. This final chapter is the essence of the Upanishadic texts, such as *Katha* and *Svetashvatara;* Tantric texts such as *Saundaryalahari* and *Tantraloka;* and the sayings and stories of the sages from the traditions of Shankaracharya and Guru Gorakh Nath. It shows how to work toward receiving, retaining, and multiplying the grace of God without falling into a cult.

Constant contemplation and reflection on the material in this book (which was completed in the form of a spiritual diary in the fall of 1993) enabled me to better understand the problems I was witnessing in spiritual seekers as well as many of my own unresolved riddles. It also helped me gain a better understanding (although there is still much to understand) of what my gurudeva meant when he repeatedly said, "Do not use the guru as a crutch. The guru is like a boat, and it is important for the boat not to leak. If you do not know how to row your boat, it is neither the fault of the boat nor of the river. If you successfully crossed the river with the help of the boat, you may not need to carry the boat with you, but neither do you need to destroy it."

Ordinarily we spend so much time brooding about such issues as the benefits and pitfalls of gurus, traditions, mantra, God, and *shaktipata* that we have hardly any time left for actually studying and practicing. It is my wish that reading this book will help spiritual seekers conquer their internal enemies without wasting too much of their time and energy, and thus reach the other shore of life safely.

In the beginning was the Word,

and the Word was with God,

and the Word was God. . . .

And the Word was made flesh,

and dwelt among us, . . .

full of grace and truth.

John 1:1,14

THE BRIDGE TO THE INNER WORLD

W̶e all want peace and happiness. The search to find peace and happiness underlies all of our endeavors, worldly as well as spiritual. We busy ourselves seeking money, power, and position—hoping they will bring us peace and happiness. Sometimes they do, at least for a while. But acquisitions and achievements are like a gourmet meal—the pleasure and sense of satisfaction quickly fade, and we are hungry again. According to the sages, the fragments of joy we find in the external world are a reflection of the boundless joy that is our birthright, the heritage of our eternal home. When we are born, they say, we bring a wisp of that joy with us. As William Wordsworth put it:

> Not in entire forgetfulness,
> And not in utter nakedness,
> But trailing clouds of glory do we come
> From God, who is our home.
>
> _Ode. Intimations of Immortality_

Because we have not entirely forgotten this home, we move restlessly through the world, hoping to find a way back. For until we do, we cannot experience real joy. Even when we are surrounded by family and friends, even when we have achieved material comfort and recognition, we are still haunted by an underlying sense of loneliness, an indefinable sense that something is missing. We try everything we can think of to banish this sense, but even if we manage to stifle it, it always returns. Eventually we stop trying and resign ourselves to life as it is. Our life runs its course, and we depart—empty and disappointed.

This is the experience of most people. However, those who are endowed with good karmas, the company of the wise, and God's grace are not discouraged by the ultimate emptiness of all that makes up the external world. Instead, they recognize it as a fact, and look elsewhere for inner fulfillment, standing firm in the midst of the hollow temptations and distractions of worldly life. Armed with firm determination, inner strength, self-trust, and fearlessness, these seekers confront their karmic challenges, pay them off, wash them off, or burn them in the fire of knowledge, eventually attaining freedom from the forces that bind them to the mundane world. For such people the realization that this world is painful and ultimately unfulfilling yields a determination to move from pain to joy, from the lower reality to the higher reality.

Once underway, this transition can be completed quickly. Adepts tell us, "Just turn your face and you are there." Unfortunately, because many of us have developed a firm belief that the world we perceive through our senses is the real world, we find it difficult to turn away from it. Although we may find the high ideals of spirituality and mysticism compelling, they are, after all, only ideals—we have no way to actualize them in our life, no way to move from the realm of transitory pain and pleasure to the realm of eternal joy. A vast chasm seems to stretch between the outer world and the inner world. We feel the pull of the inner realm, but have no way to cross from here to there. For that we need a bridge. We also need to find our way to that bridge, and for this we may need help. Then, when we do find the bridge, we discover that we cannot cross without the guidance of someone who has perfect understanding of this world and the world beyond, and who also knows the nature of the bridge.

Before we can accept guidance, however, we must be certain of the wisdom and compassion of the guide. We must be fully convinced that he or she is a balanced and lawful citizen of both worlds. Most people either are immersed in the world of lower reality and are unaware of the higher spiritual realm, or they are so established in the divine Self that they are not aware of the external world. Those who are here and there simultaneously are *siddhas*—that is, accomplished masters. They stand between the two worlds, occasionally sharing their higher knowledge with those living in the realm of lower reality. But because they are half here and half there, their words and actions may not be entirely comprehensible for most of us. They are often misunderstood because we cannot comprehend how someone can be like us, and yet entirely different. Throughout history we have persecuted such masters, recognizing them as prophets and saints only after they have shed their mortal bodies. Enlightened souls like Moses, Krishna, and Christ were not recognized while they walked among us in the flesh.

Fortunately, we have nevertheless been blessed with the presence of saints and sages who have made their home on the other shore but who still choose to sojourn among us—in the full knowledge that most of us fail to recognize them. Out of compassion for our helplessness, they have built a bridge between the two worlds and offer guidance to those who choose to cross it. Every culture has its own stories of these selfless, compassionate souls who lived only for the sake of others. Some still live among us, even today. Our problem is learning to recognize them. If they live and behave as we do, we don't notice them. If they behave peculiarly, we dismiss them as strange or crazy, or write them off as showoffs, or perhaps even dangerous. We recognize them when we meet them only when we ourselves have developed a certain purity of intention.

STARTING OUT

In the beginning stages of our quest, we do not need a perfect master who has complete knowledge of this world, the world beyond, and the bridge connecting them. We need only a sound philosophy of life and systematic techniques for improving our physical, mental, and spiritual well-being in order to develop the clarity for starting our journey in earnest. We need guidance from books and instructors so we can begin to develop an understanding of the spiritual realm and gain the necessary skill to read the map that will lead us there.

Practicing the techniques will help us identify our strengths and weaknesses.

We do not need an accomplished master to lead us to the bridge between the two realms. An instructor or manual can show us the way. Even common sense may be enough. Many roads lead to this bridge. The one that is best is the one that suits our particular circumstances, physical capacity, emotional maturity, and intellectual grasp. But no matter which route we take, it merges with all other roads just this side of the bridge. There, we find our access blocked by two powerful barriers: fear and skepticism.

The fear stems from the knowledge that we must now leave the road that brought us to the bridge. We have formed strong attachments to our cultural background and religious upbringing. The thought of leaving this familiar domain and moving into the unknown is frightening. Throughout the early stages of the journey we were certain that reaching the other shore and attaining immortal bliss was the highest goal of life. But now that we have reached the jumping-off point we find that attachment to the empty experiences we have gathered so painfully, together with fear of the unknown, are arguing fiercely for turning around and returning to the realm of the familiar. "Perhaps that life isn't so meaningless after all," we say. "At least I know what's there and who I am in that world. If I go back and try harder, maybe I'll find something of real value there. I can always come back here and cross this bridge later."

The only way to conquer fear is to conquer skepticism, the second obstacle. Skepticism has a host of telling arguments.

"Who knows that this is the right bridge?" "I might have taken the wrong turn." "I'm sure there are other bridges. Even if this is the right bridge, how do I know if it is sturdy? It looks fragile. Many bridges have been known to collapse under the weight of travelers."

Skepticism stems from lack of faith, lack of belief in the existence of a higher truth, and inability to trust what is said by the scriptures and saints. But anything in the world can be doubted and contradicted. If we understand this, we can overcome skepticism. For instance, try doubting the skepticism: Why should the scriptures and the sages throughout the ages try to deceive and misguide others? Why do they all say the same thing regardless of their time and place in history? Isn't it likely that somewhere, at some time, there was at least one person who was totally selfless, compassionate, and kind, at least one person who did not guide others with ill intention?

If we do not overcome them, fear and skepticism will force us to abandon the idea of crossing to the other shore. And if we bring them along with us, they could easily manifest when we are already on the bridge, causing us to indulge in an emotional outburst and jump into the chasm. This is why overcoming fear and skepticism in the early stages is so important. The bridge is there, but unless our mind and heart are clear and strong, we will never succeed in crossing.

Knowing what the bridge is will help us overcome the obstacles. So what is it? All traditions—ancient and modern, Eastern and Western—answer in one voice: the Word. The Word is the bridge between the immanent and the transcendent, between the manifest and the unmanifest. Using divine words as the bridge, seekers from all times and traditions have completed their journeys from individual to cosmic, from mundane to divine, from short-lived pleasure to everlasting joy, from intellect to intuition, and from personal to impersonal reality.

THE WORD THROUGHOUT HISTORY AND ACROSS CULTURES

The concept of the Word and its transformative power is universal. It is found everywhere: among the Karadjeri of Australia; among the Dogon and Igbo communities of Africa; in Chamula, the Mayan community of Mexico; among the Sumerians; in the Kabalah; in the Vedic and Tantric traditions; and in Buddhism, Sufism, Christianity, and Islam. Each tradition recognizes that there is an aspect of language—the Word—that is a manifestation of the Supreme Being, or Absolute Truth. This is not a metaphor—the Word is not a means of communicating with the sacred realm; it is itself the Absolute Truth.

Many of these traditions hold that the sacred word or sound is the fundamental force behind the manifestation of the universe. For example, according to the Dogon, words uttered during religious ceremonies contain *nyama* (the life-force), which is conveyed by the breath and flows through the mouth of a holy person. This life-force unites with the life-force of the gods being evoked, and awakens the life-sustaining energy of sacrificial offerings made to nature so that it can assimilate and multiply the energy for the benefit of all humankind. The

Dogon believe that the life-force contained in the Word is transmitted to human beings by a snake deity and it is through the creative power of the Word that God fertilizes the cosmic egg in the beginning of creation.

The people of the Igbo community believe that the name of God is too sacred to be spoken by impure tongues; instead, they use the phrase "the one whose name is not spoken." Among the Chamula of Mexico, the sacred words recited during ritual worship are different from the words spoken in daily life. They are believed to contain fire. The gods consume this fire and are appeased by the shining heat of the sacred words.

The texts of ancient Sumeria also describe the creative power of the Divine Word. According to them, the universe begins to evolve as the thought of creation arises in the minds of the gods. In response to this thought, they pronounce a name, and instantly the corresponding objects come into existence. A similar concept of creation is found in the Bible. In Genesis, for example, God establishes law and order and brings about existence in its manifest form simply by utterance: "In the beginning God created the heaven and the earth. And the earth was without form, and void; and darkness was upon the face of the deep. And the Spirit of God moved upon the face of the waters. And God said, Let there be light: and there was light" (Genesis 1:1-3).

In the Kabalah, the medieval tradition of Jewish mysticism, we find a remarkable description of the nature of the Divine Word and how it springs forth from transcendental Truth. According to the Kabalah, God is transcendent and formless.

From God flows a series of ten emanations of light (*sefirot*). God cannot be known, only the light of God. Parallel to this stream of light, the divine language also unfolds, eventually condensing into the form of the twenty-two phonemes of the Hebrew language. Just as in the yogic tradition, in which *nada* and *bindu* (sound and light) manifest together, here in the tradition of the Kabalah, sound manifests alongside light.

The Word is the core of spirituality in the Judeo-Christian tradition as well. Moses reached the highest rung of the spiritual ladder when "the Lord descended in the cloud, and stood with him there, and proclaimed the name of the Lord" (Exodus 34:5). In the New Testament, Christ says, "The sower soweth the word. . . . but when they have heard, Satan cometh immediately, and taketh away the word that was sown in their hearts. . . . And these are they which are sown on good ground; such as hear the word, and receive it, and bring forth fruit, some thirtyfold, some sixty, and some an hundred" (Mark 4:14-15, 20) and "Blessed are they that hear the word of God, and keep it" (Luke 11:28) and "Now ye are clean through the word which I have spoken unto you" (John 15:3). As we will see later, when God proclaims his name, it has great spiritual significance. When people hear the Word, and receive it, and keep it, they are purified.

A Vedic sage, Ambhrini, recounts her experience of oneness with the power of the Word, which she attained during the state of spiritual absorption:

It is I who move along with prominent gods Rudra,
Vasu, Vishvadeva.

21

I uphold law and order. I sustain the day and night and I fulfill the desires of the seekers. I am the provider of prosperity, and I am the eye of the seers.

I assume numerous forms. I penetrate the earth and again grow in the form of grains and vegetables.

I am the breath of the one who breathes. I am the power of hearing of the hearers.

Independent of any other force, I utter the words. Served by wise ones I materialize the objects of their desires.

I stretch the string of the bow held in the hands of Rudra. I dispel the darkness of ignorance.

I pervade and permeate the whole universe.

It is through my glory the unmanifest becomes manifest.

Rig Veda 10:125.1-8

According to Tantric and Vedic sources, the world manifests from the Word, exists in the Word, and at the time of annihilation returns to the Word. They tell us that for those who are unaware of the power of the Word and its binding and releasing force, this world is the source of pain and misery. Yet, according to the *Shiva Sutra*, this same world is a wave of joy to those who have penetrated the mystery of the Word. Again: while giving final instruction to his chosen disciple, the siddha master Guru Gorakh Nath says, "The Word is the lock and the Word is the key. An awakened Word, received from an awakened master, is the only way to awaken the dormant Word in the heart of the sleeping disciple. Upon introducing the Word, the gross articulate word merges into the eternal Word" (*Gorakhabani 21*).

An intriguing aspect of the sacred Word is that it manifests its power only if it is proclaimed or uttered by one who has the capacity to do so. For example, in the Old Testament we find God revealing His power by proclaiming His name to Moses, and in the Indian tradition the names of Lord Rama and Lord Krishna unfold their divine nature only after the sages Vashishtha and Garga pronounce them.

Buddhist scriptures also embody the concept of the sacred Word. There, the Bodhisattva, or Buddha, is the source of grace and emancipation. Like Jesus, he is a savior; human beings can reach him by calling his name. Explaining how the name of Buddha carries the power of communication between mundane and sacred, between this world and the transcendental, Buddhist scriptures tell us that Amitabha Buddha, in his previous life as the Bodhisattva, uttered a solemn vow that suffering souls who have fallen in the cycle of birth and death could reach him through the name "Amitabha." Only an evolved soul like Buddha can utter a word and assign power to it with unfailing effect; the vow and its effects are embodied literally in the Word he utters. Consequently, many people in China repeat the name of Amitabha Buddha as part of their spiritual practice, deriving inner fulfillment from it.

In the esoteric tradition of the Japanese Tantra founded by Kukai (774–835 A.D.), all words, especially Sanskrit sounds, are considered to be the embodiment of the highest reality. In the Islamic and Sufi traditions, the Word (*Kalam*) of Allah is eternal: "These expressions which are spoken and are heard

23

[when the Qur'an is being read] are the Word of the Most High." It is also said that God has a thousand names (which is a way of indicating an infinite number), and only God knows them all. In the yoga tradition, especially among the Tantrics, reciting the thousand names of a god or goddess is an essential part of spiritual practice.

THE WORD IS THE BRIDGE

Unless we have at least a rudimentary understanding of the metaphysics of sound, its eternity (the power of speech), and its source (the vibrant energy of the tranquil truth), we cannot grasp the mystery of the divine names and the manner in which they form a bridge between the two worlds. This is the essence of mantra science. It can be understood only when we are able to distinguish between intellectual knowledge and intuitive wisdom. Crossing this bridge, with resolution born of utter conviction, is possible only when we understand how the Divine Word can lead individual consciousness to reunion with Supreme Consciousness. This understanding is rooted in an understanding of the difference between mundane and divine language and how the power of the Word flows from the Source and is received in varying degrees.

The face of Truth is covered by a golden veil. O Thou Power of Protection and Nourishment, reveal that Truth to the one who seeks it sincerely.

Isha Upanishad, verse 15

BLOCKING AND UNVEILING THE LIGHT

Words are of two kinds—mundane and divine—and they emerge from two different realms—the external and the internal. Mundane words are vibrations perceived by our ears which our minds interpret as words. We call sounds "words" only if there is an established relationship between the sound and the object indicated. Just as there are an infinite number of objects and vibratory sound patterns, so there are an infinite number of words, all of which have their origin in sound waves.

The Divine Word originates from itself. It is nondual, transcendental Truth that chooses to manifest in the form of the Word. The mystical schools of all spiritual traditions acknowledge that the flow of divine light takes the form of sacred words. For example, according to the Kabalah, the Torah is the mystical name of God. "The Divine Energy chose to articulate itself in the form of the letters of the Torah as they express themselves in God's name. On the one hand, this name comprises the Divine Potency; on the other hand it comprehends within it the totality of the concealed laws of creation."

The Divine Word is like the sun. As the intrinsic nature of our inner self, it is always shining. Mundane words, the language and din of worldly concerns, are like fog rising from a valley. The denser the fog, the harder it is to see the sun's brilliance from the valley floor. Fog often obstructs the light in early morning, but as the sun gets hotter and its light more intense, it burns away the fog and becomes visible in its full glory. The less fog we manufacture, the greater our chances of receiving revelation in the form of the Word.

The Divine Word is known only to those who understand its universal language, which is the language of the soul. At the soul level, we speak and hear only the Word. Our confusion—our fog—arises at the level of body, senses, mind, ego, and intellect. Our thoughts, speech, and actions collide, making our mind so noisy that the inner voice is drowned out. Lowering the volume of worldly noise and directing our attention to the divine whisper within is *sadhana* (spiritual practice). Through *sadhana* we develop the ability to minimize mental and emotional static, making it possible for the voice of the soul, the Word, to reveal itself to us.

THE MIND AS MEANS OR IMPEDIMENT

Mental and emotional noise is created by the sensory data we take in and how these data are stored in our mental field. If the incoming sensory data are not disturbing and if they are received and stored properly, the mental field remains quiet and steady. On the other hand, when we involve ourselves in disturbing actions, when we cram a jumble of jolting experiences into our thoughts and memories, the mind field, which stands between individual consciousness and the universal consciousness, becomes polluted. A polluted, confused mind reflects a distorted picture of inner truth, whereas a pure, steady mind reflects reality accurately, creating the conditions both for a successful life in the external world and for the dawning of spiritual understanding. Thus, the scriptures describe the mind as the cause of both bondage and liberation.

The mind is not the source of revelation, but it has the power to veil revealed knowledge, filtering and distorting it in the process. The *Yoga Sutra* identifies five states of mind: disturbed, distracted, stupefied, one-pointed, and well-controlled. These states determine how we respond to the external world and how external circumstances influence our internal world. In the first three states, the mind is confused. A confused mind is not an effective tool in either worldly or spiritual endeavors; people with confused minds can help neither themselves nor others. What is more, revealed knowledge cannot penetrate the fog created by a confused mind. For this reason, it is crucial to calm the mind and render it one-pointed. Only then can the sunlight of Truth penetrate our awareness, infusing it with revealed knowledge.

THE DESCENT OF LIGHT

Light is the intrinsic nature of the absolute Truth. It radiates unceasingly in all directions, illuminating all that is. Nothing can be apprehended, nothing can exist without the light of the Truth. The mind's power to think, feel, analyze, and decide has its source in Divine Light. The brain, the nervous system, the organs, and limbs of the body derive their capacities from the Light. As long as the Divine Light dwells in us, we are animated. The moment it is withdrawn, we cease to exist. Although the Light is always within us, the mind stands between it and our individual consciousness.

Because everything in the world is known through Divine Light, direct realization of the Light bestows knowledge of all that exists, both manifest and unmanifest. Revelation is the direct experience of Divine Light. Revelation is always complete—there is no such thing as higher revelation or lower revelation. However, the Light of inner being penetrates our consciousness in varying degrees of intensity, depending on the density of the mind. Like all light, it is brightest closest to its source. As the rays travel outward, they strike our karmic and mental impurities. The more impurities, the greater the blockage. The greater the blockage, the dimmer the light is when it reaches the mind field. That is why it is said that the Divine Light flows forth in three different stages. In the scriptures these three stages of revelation are known as *prajna*, *pratibha*, and *medha* or *dhi*.

Prajna—the first level of revelation—is the pure and perfect spontaneous knowledge of Truth in its entirety. *Prajna* is not the knowledge of something in relation to something else, but the experience of union, the realization of truth in its perfection and purity. A yogi blessed with *prajna* experiences complete oneness with the highest Truth. "My Father and I are one" is an expression of *prajna*. In yogic literature, a sage blessed with this level of revelation is called a *brahmarishi*.

The second stage of revelation, *pratibha*, is unimaginable intellectual revelation or genius. At this stage, an aspect of truth is known in its totality and perfection. *Pratibha* may also involve instantaneous intuitive knowledge. It is a flash rather than a continuous flow of inner light. A yogi blessed with *pratibha* does not experience oneness with the highest truth, but rather has a sense of being a "seer" and "seeing" the revealed knowledge. Experientially, it is as though the realm of time is transcended and a major aspect of knowledge unfolds. Newton's comprehension of the law of gravity while watching an apple fall is an example of this type of revelation. Although the law of gravity was revealed to him, he did not experience his oneness with that law. Rather, the revelation came in the form of objective awareness. Even while it was taking place, Newton as an individual consciousness was totally separate from it. Further, the revelation was not complete—numberless other mysteries remained veiled.

The third stage of revelation, *medha* or *dhi,* takes the form of retentive power—the ability of the mind to store its experiences. Although the inner light is not as powerful here as in the first two stages, it is bright enough to illuminate experiences occurring in a wider realm than our awareness normally encompasses. For example, suppose you are struggling to solve a mathematical problem, but getting nowhere. Suddenly, the answer flashes in your mind. In a strict sense, this is not an intuitive revelation, but the result of the concentrated force of your inner awareness. This inner awareness helped you to gain access to a point in time and to a place with which you were already familiar. In other words, this level of revelation creates an internal environment where the focus of the mind becomes so condensed and penetrating that suddenly the experiences of the past burned in the bed of memory are brought to the conscious level.

This third stage of revelation provides constant guidance to the *buddhi* (intellect). Intellect is the mind's decisive faculty; it compares, contrasts, judges, verifies, and decides. The intellect makes decisions based on its previous experiences and is guided by the voice of the soul. But if the retentive power is dim, the intellect functions poorly. It does not know what to base its decisions on nor how to make sure that those decisions are congruent with one another. An intellect only weakly illumined by *medha* lacks confidence and is doomed to indecision. It fails to provide right counseling to the ego when conflicts arise; thus the ego acts blindly. A dull intellect and a blind ego fail to provide proper direction to the lower mind—the aspect of the mind that works in coordination with the senses. The lower mind and senses then busy themselves running about in the external world, creating confusion, insecurity, and fear.

BLOCKING THE LIGHT

Revelation comes from within. Everyone is endowed with the inner light from which *prajna, pratibha,* and *medha* radiate, but due to the conditions created by the mind, ego, intellect, and unconscious, most of us fail to perceive that light. The mental and karmic impurities have formed a crust so thick that the Light of Truth cannot penetrate it, and we find ourselves without access to the inner light. All we can do is work with the mind and shed as many impurities as possible.

This requires effort—self-effort. No one else can work with our mind for us. No teacher or therapist can clean our mind, remove the confusion, and make it one-pointed. Self-therapy and self-help are the only solutions. Further, this clean-up project must begin from where we are, from our current state. For most of us, that means beginning with our body because we are so externally oriented that our awareness is largely confined to our physical existence.

Much of our activity is centered around our body. Most of our actions are attempts to find pleasure and to avoid discomfort and pain. Pursuing physical pleasure leads to stress and emotional injury and causes toxins to accumulate—all of which affect the mind. That is why the process of cleansing the impurities from the mind must begin at the level of the body. A healthy body is the embarkation point for the journey to the center of our being. The foundation of a fruitful spiritual practice consists of eating healthy food, getting the proper exercise, regulating the breath, moderating our sleep habits, and exercising restraint in the area of sense gratification. [See Appendix A: Preparation for Mantra Initiation.]

As our body becomes healthier, our awareness becomes more refined and we encounter increasingly subtle impurities in the various layers of our mind. Although there are an endless number and variety, these impurities fall into five basic categories:

◆Scatteredness or lack of focus, which impairs the functioning of the mind;

◆Doubts and complexes, which affect the ego;

◆Indecisiveness, which weakens the intellect;

◆ *Vasanas* (karmic impurities), which have an adverse effect on the unconscious mind; and

◆Killing the conscience, which undermines the retentive power.

Systematic spiritual practice gradually attenuates these impurities. Meditation is the antidote to the first three because it overcomes scatteredness and brings the mind to a state of one-pointedness. The less scattered the mind, the clearer the perception. The clearer the perception, the fewer doubts and complexes entangle the ego. The less entangled the ego, the less it interferes with the decisive faculty of the intellect. An ego ensnared in complexes continually interferes with the functioning of the intellect, making it impossible to sort information correctly, leading to indecisiveness. By providing an antidote to scatteredness, meditation washes away the impurities that pollute the mind, ego, and intellect.

Karmic impurities affect the unconscious mind and can be washed off by practicing non-attachment *(vairagya)*. Non-attachment arises from the awareness that nothing in this world really belongs to us and that the objects of the world are not the highest goal of life. Applying this knowledge in daily life helps us stop identifying ourselves with thoughts and memories deposited in the unconscious mind. Thus, when our karmic impurities resurface in the form of memories, we no longer identify with them and can let them pass without being affected.

The fifth category of impurity—killing the conscience—weakens the retentive power. The Light of Truth in the form of conscience constantly tells us what is right and what is wrong. Nevertheless, driven by our attachments, desires, and habits, we fail to do that which we are supposed to do and continue doing that which we are not supposed to do. Because we do this with full awareness of what is right and what is wrong, conflict arises between the voice of the soul and the uncontrolled urges of the mind. We know that it is best to heed the voice of the soul, but we comply instead with the demands of the mind. This causes guilt and self-condemnation, which in turn kills the conscience. To cope with our guilt, we hide ourselves from the Light. The ever-flowing Light does not turn away from us; rather, we deliberately try to hide so that the Light doesn't illuminate our actions and remind us what is right and what is wrong. When we hide from the Light, the inner chamber of the heart becomes dark and we cannot see our reflection in the mirror of our own mind. This is frightening. We begin to forget who we are, and retentive power begins to drain away. Once begun, this process accelerates from the force of its own momentum.

When the retentive power becomes dim, forgetfulness sets in. We no longer know who we are. We may not even remember the Light and, even if we do, we cannot remember how it relates to us. The ego takes over. Because the decisive faculty of the higher intellect has also been cut off from the inner illumination provided by the retentive power, the ego uses the mind to conjure up self-deceptive tricks. An unillumined intellect has little control over an ego and mind so engaged and becomes subservient to both. The mind behaves like a magician and begins to entertain the ego; in turn, the ego begins to claim that it is the lord of life. Thus the worldly cycle is set in motion—getting into bondage and attempting to gain liberation—and it all occurs in darkness. According to yogis, this is the dark night of the soul.

THE CONFUSION OF TONGUES

Most of the human race is immersed in the dark night of the soul. While so immersed we create and accumulate so many karmas and karmic impurities that they block the Light completely. In the darkness we begin to build a tower of desires, attachment, anger, hatred, jealousy, and greed. By the time this tower is completed, we have forgotten the universal language. In the absence of the Light of Truth, we mistake this tower of ego for a magnificent monument and begin fighting among ourselves for exclusive possession. To strengthen our positions, to maintain our identities, and to hold on to our possessions we make common cause with others and create a group identity. In the process, we develop a language that is comprehensible only to members of "our" group.

The languages we invent while fighting at the tower of ego are thick with confusion. They do not flow from the realm of Truth and clarity but from the domain of selfishness and fear. These languages do not have the spontaneous power of that universal language which is spoken and heard by the soul.

Because they are constructed by superimposing meaning on specific sounds and can be understood only by our own group, they are extremely limited and do not have the power to express the higher truths clearly. The Bible refers to this confusion of tongues as the Tower of Babel.

When we have built and fortified the tower of ego and discarded the universal language in favor of a confused dialect, we are no longer able to perceive the Light of Truth. Revelation is no longer an option because its subtle rays cannot penetrate the thick walls of ego. In the language of the religionists, this is the original fall from grace.

THE DESCENT OF LIGHT AS SOUND

According to Vedic and Tantric scriptures, *rishis,* the seers of the mantras, either never experienced this fall from grace or, having fallen, overcame the confusion of the tongues. In either case, these seers have described how the Light of Truth illuminates every aspect of existence both within and without. We have already touched on their description of how the Divine Light flows in three successive stages (*prajna, pratibha,* and *dhi*). The light they describe is not like the physical light which we see through our eyes; rather, it is the light of knowledge that unveils the mystery of the unknown and unseen. Simultaneously with the manifestation of the Divine Light, the Divine Sound also manifests in three successive stages: *pashyanti, madhyama,* and *vaikhari.*

Pashyanti is the highest stage. Here the Word contains the pure and perfect knowledge of truth. At this stage, the Word does not manifest in an articulate sound but is a state of pure awareness just verging on seeing what is there to be seen. *Pashyanti* means "the power that is in the process of seeing." At this stage the objective world is in a state of divine ideation, a state of self-affirmation: "I am this and I could be that." *Pashyanti* contains the potentials of all the words and their meanings and is experienced only in deep *samadhi*, spiritual absorption. The saints and scriptures use mystical language to describe this mystical state. "Without hearing, the hearer hears, while hearing, the hearer never hears."

At the stage of *pashyanti*, the Divine Word is called *shruti*, "that which is heard." But the one who "hears" it is called *rishi*, "the seer," rather than the hearer. At this stage of revelation, the seer becomes one with the Word in the same way that a sage blessed with *prajna* experiences oneness with the highest Truth. In this context it is said that the knower of Brahman becomes Brahman, and the knower of mantra becomes mantra. The words of the Vedas were "heard" by the seers at the stage of *pashyanti* while they were in profound spiritual trance. That is why every single letter, word, and sentence of the Vedas is considered to be a form of revelation.

In *madhyama,* the second stage, the Word does not contain the pure and perfect knowledge of the entire range of truth; rather it contains a clear knowledge of one aspect of the truth. This is the Word that is a vehicle for genius; it corresponds to *pratibha. Madhyama* is a form of intellectual revelation in which the word is not yet articulate, although it has formulated a thought pattern. It is a kind of non-verbal thinking process in which the power of thought is so concentrated and so absorbing that the thinker does not attend to the words being used as vehicles for thinking. From amid this concentrated flow of thought, a tremendous amount of information suddenly comes forth in an intuitive flash. Yet at this stage, the Word remains unarticulated.

It reaches the realm of articulation only in *vaikhari,* the third stage. Here the Word is a locus for retentive power and enables the mind to store and express its experiences. In the mundane realm, we assign a word to every bit of knowledge and experience, and use these words to store information. Similiarly, in the spiritual realm our learning process operates at the level of words. On the surface, mantra initiation is given at the level of *vaikhari:* a mantra is spoken by a teacher and heard by a student. If the mantra comes from the source, sooner or later it will lead the consciousness of the meditator toward the source. On the way back, as it passes through the progressively more subtle stages of *madhyama* and *pashyanti,* a meditator will hear the same word at a different frequency.

According to the seers of the Vedas and the mystics of the Kabalah, every syllable of the Vedas and the Torah is a focus of revealed knowledge, a focal point from which Divine Light emanates. Because we lack *divya chakshu* (divine eyesight) and *divya shrota* (divine ears), we neither see the Light nor hear the Divine Words emanating from these scriptures. Yet as we practice Vedic mantras or the Torah, we move toward a higher level of purity and preparedness. At some point we will begin to perceive Divine Light and the words that flash forth from these revealed scriptures. That is the experience of the Divine Word at the level of *madhyama*. As this process deepens, the practitioner becomes totally one with those revealed scriptures and the Divine Word is heard intuitively at the level of *pashyanti*, the source of all mantras.

The Divine Word emerges from the Source and has a tendency to return to the Source. The pure-hearted sages receive it and remain connected with it. They dwell in the Word and the Word dwells in them. They become one with the Word and with each other. Out of compassion, the Word flows from their pure tongues, enters the heart of other fortunate seekers, and performs the miracle of connecting them to the source, just as it did in the case of the first seer. In the living lineage of a spiritual tradition, this process continues from generation to generation. That is how these revealed words—mantras—are heard, received, treasured, and passed on.

No one who receives a mantra from a master who is part of a living lineage will wander helplessly through the wilderness of worldly life. The mantra knows where its real abode is and only travels in that direction. If we receive the mantra and hold it in our mind and heart, we will reach our true home.

In the sahasrara chakra there lies

an inverted well brimming with

the elixir of immortality. One

who is guided by a guru drinks it

to his fill, but one who is not so

guided goes thirsty.

Gorakh Bani, verse 23

FINDING A TEACHER

Words spoken by a confused tongue will confuse the mind of the person who hears them. Conversely, words uttered by the pure tongue of an enlightened being will purify the mind of anyone receiving them. Knowledge of the doctrine of revelation is not enough—only the direct experience of revelation can give us inner fulfillment. Once the desire for revelation is kindled the question becomes, "How can we receive revelation? And from whom?" Only one who has attained inner illumination can guide us on the path of Light, and only one who has received the Divine Word can pass it on to others in the form of mantra. But how can we find such a person? And do we need to?

THE NEED FOR A TEACHER

People wonder whether they really need a teacher, especially when they consider the difficulties involved in finding one who is both competent and trustworthy. There is so much information on spiritual practice, meditation, and mantras available in books and magazines that these sources may seem sufficient. After all, the spiritual quest involves overcoming our own delusion and unfolding our own inner potential. Even the scriptures tell us, "Light your own lamp—no one else can give you enlightenment." So why not simply find our own way?

Although it is true that anything, including enlightenment, can be obtained without anyone's help, help really helps! In any field of knowledge, a proven system of education is valuable. In a system that has been developed by trial and error over time, a series of experiments has established the validity of its method; it has been applied repeatedly and found to yield similar results time after time. A proven method of education is the most direct route to any form of knowledge. Charting our own path is time-consuming, especially when a map is available. This is true whether the goal is mastery of the violin, medicine, quantum physics, architecture, gymnastics—or spirituality. In any learning endeavor, the combination of a teacher and a proven method enables the student to learn systematically and to avoid pitfalls. Without such guidance, students must search here and there, going down blind alleys, wandering off the trail, and falling into confusion. They may never stumble onto a system of learning that works for them and, even if they do, they will have wasted valuable time, even, perhaps, forfeiting the possibility of gaining mastery.

In spirituality, as in other fields, it is far better to study and practice under the guidance of a mentor or teacher—someone who has assimilated the experiences of previous seekers and explorers and used those experiences to attain a high level of skill and knowledge. A true teacher has received instructions and guidance from his own mentor, undertaken and mastered a course of study and practice, and integrated the wisdom gleaned along the way. Such a teacher has a depth of knowledge that qualifies him to help us find the method, complete with shortcuts, that works best for us.

But how can we find the right teacher without making too many mistakes? The answer is simple: you find what you look for. As the Bible tells us, "Ask, and it shall be given you; seek, and ye shall find; knock, and it shall be opened unto you" (Matthew 7:7). But the Bible doesn't tell us how many times to knock or even where to find the door. The truth is that if we begin our search with full determination, then instinct, intuition, destiny, karma—whatever term you prefer—will guide us to the door. Similar attracts similar. This is a universal law. In the natural course of events there will come a time when we begin wondering, "Where am I going? Where have I come from? What is the purpose of my life?" As these questions become stronger and more persistent, worldly charms begin to lose their luster, and we begin to move toward the door.

We need not find the right place or the right person in our first attempt. As we shall see, the path to the final door—mantra initiation—is not necessarily a straight line. In the beginning, we will find books, courses, or instructors who inspire us. They may not have the ultimate answer, but they can help us gain the clarity to see our next step.

Most of us seek direct guidance from a teacher under one of four circumstances. The first is desperation. We have come to realize that life is full of pain and misery. We have tried to find lasting happiness in every way we know, and nothing has worked. Therapy, counseling, religious formulas, and other forms of professional help have left us unfulfilled. We are troubled by life's problems and ready to try anything.

The second circumstance is curiosity. We don't know enough to have a clear idea of where the truth lies or how to find it, but we do know enough to be curious about its unknown dimensions. This compels us to search for a way of being that is more fulfilling than the one we already know. Instead of being pushed toward spirituality by the troubling issues of worldly life, we are pulled by the possibility of something delightful ahead.

The third reason for seeking a teacher is the desire for material success. We are motivated by desire and expectation—we are hoping to get some help from above in attaining material prosperity or power—but at least we have enough sense to seek help from someone or something wiser than we are. Although this is not a superb starting point, it does lead us in the direction of the company of the wise. Sooner or later it will bear fruit.

The fourth circumstance in which we seek a teacher is the search for knowledge. When we have seen how short-lived and empty worldly pleasures are, we often turn to philosophical and spiritual texts for the answers. On the intellectual level we are convinced that there is a higher truth, and we come to a teacher seeking to experience this truth for ourselves.

Most of us begin our effort to find a teacher under one of

the first three circumstances, and our quest is half-hearted because we are not looking for truth so much as we are seeking to solve our worldly problems. Then, when our desperation has abated, or our curiosity has been satisfied, or we have come to realize that our worldly desires will not be fulfilled in the way we had hoped, we may lose interest. Despite this, sometimes the spiritual vibrations we have experienced in our initial quest—no matter how impure, misguided, or quixotic that quest may be—are powerful enough to set us irretrievably on a spiritual course, and thenceforth our life becomes a slow but sure process of self-transformation. The path of those rare seekers who come to a teacher with the burning desire for pure knowledge is straighter and more direct, but even they sometimes fall into the trap of identifying so strongly with their knowledge that they never come to understand its limitations.

No matter the reason for our search, finding a teacher takes time. Even if we are fortunate enough to meet the right one immediately, he may not give us what we had expected. The teacher is not bound to fulfill our expectations. In fact, a teacher who has undergone training with a competent master knows the importance of teaching only what is best for us, and that may not be what we are expecting. But even though our immediate expectations may not be met, the first encounter with our teacher makes an enormous impression on our mind and heart. Intellectually we may not be impressed, but deep down we feel blessed by his company. And this kindles the desire to learn something from that person.

This first meeting is crucial. In the first instant we recognize one another, not with our eyes or through a formal introduction, but rather with our hearts. Two hearts meet and know each other at the level of feeling. We must catch hold of that moment of recognition, and make sure that our undisciplined and argumentative mind does not confuse us later.

A teacher gently reminds us that there is more to learn and attain. He inspires us when we condemn ourselves; when we become egotistical about the little knowledge we have already attained, he reminds us of the limitless fountain of knowledge that lies ahead. During the interaction between teacher and student, misunderstandings and doubt may arise, and occasionally the student gets fed up and leaves. If this occurs, it simply means that the student needed more courage and determination. But a teacher can give up on a student only after the student has abandoned the teacher. Even then, the teacher keeps making efforts to bring back a student who is close to the destination, but who has taken a wrong exit.

Learning and practice are an ongoing process, one that brings about a qualitative change in the relationship between teacher and student. It becomes more intimate and, as it does, a broader understanding emerges. The more we understand, the finer and more subtle the bond and, as the relationship deepens, the teacher becomes increasingly precise, straightforward, and authoritative. Eventually he may not give oral instructions at all, but rather guide the student directly. By that time, the teacher's role is that of a master.

A student also becomes more precise, knowing exactly

which questions to ask, and eventually she no longer needs many verbal instructions, delighting, rather, in receiving silent guidance directly in the cave of the heart. Such a seeker has graduated from student to disciple. We must remember that reaching this state is a gradual process, not a one-shot event, and the form it takes varies from person to person. But for the purpose of explanation, we can break this process into three phases—beginning, intermediate, and advanced—with the understanding that the lines of demarcation are not clear cut.

IN THE BEGINNING

Regardless of what brings us to seek personal guidance, most of us begin our search by reading books or listening to tapes. This initial approach to spirituality is primarily intellectual, although if we are sincere and intelligent we also figure out how to put some of this information into practice. In the process we find answers to some of our questions, but we also find new questions. So the investigation continues; we study some more, and practice some more. Eventually we realize that something is still missing, and this kindles the desire to gain a more direct experience of the information we are acquiring.

So next we may attend a lecture or a weekend seminar. In the beginning, we will probably find the teacher convincing only if the teachings are logically sound. We may feel the need to evaluate the teacher by looking at his qualifications and making assessments: How well-read is this person? How organized and convincing are his presentations? What books has he written? How accessible is he? How humorous or charming? We also evaluate the paraphernalia around the teaching process—the physical setting, the material distributed along with the lecture, the other members of the audience. The more external evidence we have that the teacher is respected and knowledgeable, the more comfortable and attracted we are.

At this stage the teacher is simply an instructor whose only obligation is to teach what he has actually practiced, to refrain from making promises, and to teach only that which is healthy and useful. If the seminar or workshop is spiritually oriented, earning a fee must not be the prime motivation. As students, our duty is discharged as long as we do not deliberately create problems for the instructor.

When we have encountered several teachers and been exposed to a variety of teachings, this level of instruction begins to lose its charm. We realize that the greater part of the Truth lies outside flyers, brochures, press releases, and media kits. We are beginning to depend more on our direct experience, and to develop an intuitive understanding about whether or not the information given us is simply a series of facts, hypotheses, and beliefs, or the embodiment of revealed wisdom. And as this intuitive understanding grows, our desire for a more refined level of knowledge grows with it. We feel that we have read enough books and have listened to enough tapes. What we want to know can be communicated only at a deeper and subtler level.

At this point, we may approach a teacher and initiate some personal interactions, although most of us remain cautious and somewhat guarded even now. Teachers understand this, and though they may be kind and compassionate, their teaching is limited to only the elementary truths. This is the most basic level of the teacher-student relationship. The relationship is casual, and the responsibilities on both sides are still quite limited. Later on, when more extensive personal interactions begin, these responsibilities grow. Then the teacher must take the student's physical capacity, intellectual grasp, and emotional maturity into consideration as he teaches. A student is expected to be straightforward with the teacher, and to be open when the teacher speaks unpleasant truths.

In many ways, this relationship must be experienced to be understood. Confusion regarding the responsibilities of teacher and student arises only when the highest standards of duty and responsibility are established too early. They are not based on a fixed set of rules, but grow naturally and spontaneously, and there is no greater delight than experiencing their spontaneous unfoldment in this unique relationship. The very presence of the question "What is whose responsibility?" shows either that the relationship has not been fully established, or that the student is in fear of establishing such a relationship.

Somewhere in the Middle

As novice seekers, we have a long list of questions. In fact, the longer the list, and the more complicated the questions, the prouder we are of our sincerity and preparedness. If we are vigilant in fostering our inner growth, these questions serve a purpose. They stimulate our mind and stir our heart, motivating us to find answers. But sooner or later we realize that if we manufacture any more questions, our head will shatter! Further, we begin to understand that answers to these questions come from the realm of the intellect and that we must find an intuitive way of finding the real answers.

After we have met a teacher and received a few personal instructions, we study and practice, and in most cases this is a positive experience. But again the charm gradually wears off. Most seekers go through many ups and downs, often feeling that the practice is not helping them. They are not completely comfortable, and are beset by a host of doubts. "I don't think this is an appropriate practice," they feel. "I need something else—a better practice, a higher one, the next step. I wonder if my teacher has already taught me all he knows?"

In the beginning, we are fully aware of the circumstances that compelled us to find a spiritual guide, to practice under his supervision, and to receive divine help. But with the passage of time, when our problems diminish, we begin to forget that we even had them. Life becomes lighter, less troublesome. We start comparing ourselves with others. We begin to notice that someone else seems to be progressing more rapidly than we are. Someone else is more inspired. More questions arise. "Why is the teacher giving more attention to that person? Why is he using a different method to guide that person? What about me?" Beset by jealousy and dissatisfaction, we begin to make unfair demands.

As these feelings enter the mind, our focus shifts from our own study and practice to watching those around us. Who else is stuck and why? Who else is being ignored? Our dissatisfaction grows into disappointment with the teacher, and we gradually drop the process of self-analysis, self-observation, self-training, self-discipline, and self-purification that we have been following. As we do, we feel an urge to examine the teacher and the tradition from which he comes. We become troubleshooters rather than spiritual seekers. At this point the same law that helped us find the teacher in the first place (you find whatever you look for) now helps us find quarrels with the teacher. If we are looking for trouble we will find it, and if we are not vigilant the process of unfoldment will stop here and we will leave, feeling confused and angry.

To overcome these obstacles that prevent us from allowing our relationship with the teacher to unfold, we must study the whole process carefully. We must find out what is really troubling us. What are we afraid of? What is the exact nature of our doubt? What makes us feel threatened and prevents us from drawing closer to our guide?

An honest evaluation will reveal that the major obstacle is nothing more than ego. Ego has a hard time accepting anything other than its own supremacy. To overcome this we must convince the ego that working with a teacher is not a matter of accepting someone as superior to us, but simply a matter of allowing someone to guide us selflessly.

We live in a world where we learn to treasure our self-identity. We are taught to work hard to preserve our belongings, regardless of how trivial they are. We are trained to live for a personal identity—to fight for it and die for it, if necessary. We cherish the notion of personal property; not only material

possessions, but also personal faith, philosophy, religion—
even a personal god, a personal mantra, and personal meditation. Holding a passport to the world of "yours and mine"
and suddenly encountering something that aims to expand our
vision beyond the boundaries of personal property can be
frightening. It takes enormous courage to face the fear of losing our familiar self-identity.

But as we commit ourselves to the path of self-transformation, we realize that the power of spirituality helps us to refine
and expand our ego by letting it become a part of higher consciousness. By permitting ourselves to learn from a teacher, we
have not placed ourselves in an inferior position. Rather, by becoming a student we are in fact allowing our ego to be nour-
ished. It even grows—but as an adult, not like a spoiled child.
It becomes humble, but not timid. It expands rather than swells.

Our second problem at this time is doubt. It comes up
strongly if we have been misguided by others in the past. If
this has occurred, we must tell ourselves that we will not allow
one failure to stop us. Even a hundred failures must not stop
us. We cannot afford to live with fear and skepticism. We need
to recognize that our previous negative experiences were at
least partially due to our blind faith, to our unclear perception,
and most important, to our lack of a definite goal. If we throw
aside these conditions and continue to search for a teacher, we
will find one. And once we have met a teacher on the ground
of a genuine search, the rest will unfold in its natural course.
We must take care to remember the circumstances under
which we came to this teacher, what our basic goals were, and

the extent to which we have achieved those goals.

If our determination is strong, and if we practice diligently, we will see gradual progress. But along the way we will probably go through periodic ups and downs, as obstacles such as ego, attachment, fear, doubt, and the rest of the retinue show up. This is natural. Over time they gradually lose their grip on us, and the duration of inner turmoil becomes shorter and less intense. A deeper understanding of life within and without unfolds. The process of transformation manifests in the form of patience and firmness in our overall character. Through self-observation and inner analysis we begin to understand this process and to see where we are in it. This in turn helps us have reasonable expectations of both the teacher and the practice.

THE FINAL FLOWERING

The level of our own transformation helps us find the next level of teaching, either from the same teacher or from someone else. There is a definite way to verify our progress: we start realizing the limited scope of intellectual learning, and we feel the need for gaining knowledge silently, through direct transmission. When we notice the shortcomings of intellectual dialogue and are drawn to the enriching flow of direct transmission, the transformation has begun. This awareness inspires us to ignore our debate-loving argumentative mind. And when we do, the longing for direct transmission intensifies.

At the outset we commit ourselves on the shaky ground of mere belief. Prior to any direct experience, the force of anticipation fuels our quest. Then, as we learn and practice, as the anticipated fruit is achieved, our belief is confirmed and trust begins to grow. Trust is based on experience; it is stronger and more refined than mere belief. When we are operating on belief we commit ourselves to learning and practicing only to the extent we are comfortable with the teacher and the teachings. Our focus is not so much on learning as on figuring out whether the theories and techniques we are hearing about are valid. If we practice a technique and the experience is positive, the next time we are more interested in learning and less interested in comparing, contrasting, testing, and validating the method. Belief gives way to trust.

When a student is operating on belief, the teacher keeps a distance, giving advice gently, and making sure not to threaten the skeptical part of the student's mind. When the teacher notices trust unfolding, he becomes more direct. The channel of communication begins to flow effortlessly from both sides. And as the student gains more profound experiences, they reinforce the trust, which gradually ripens into firm conviction. In the scriptures, conviction is called *shraddha*, pure faith, the ground on which the guru-disciple relationship unfolds.

When we are a beginner it is natural to have limited openness, for we do not want to expose ourselves to someone we do not know very well. As we advance from belief to trust, however, we are less hesitant to share the feelings in our heart with the teacher, and the teacher feels freer to share that which he holds so dear. From both sides, the joy of giving and receiving begins to flourish. This effortless sense of complete and mutual openness is the basis for the guru-disciple relationship.

Only when we realize that all the other fine people we have learned from in the past were merely instructors and teachers, while this one is our final spiritual guide, does the teacher begin to behave like a master and treat us as a disciple. When we are committed to such an extent, it becomes the master's responsibility to gather all the resources necessary for our ultimate spiritual unfoldment. The master does everything to bring us to the highest level. His greatest delight comes when we reach the summit.

From our perspective as disciple our responsibilities grow enormously, but subtly. Our duty is to serve the master by keeping his words in the innermost chamber of our heart, letting them multiply. From the perspective of the master our duty is simply to do the practices sincerely and to be happy. If the master expects anything other than spiritual growth from the student, this so-called master has not received the proper training from a qualified master. We must remember, however, that a master may well use some unpleasant methods to foster our spiritual unfoldment. And if he does, we must be ready to accept this treatment gratefully. Not all of us receive this experience—it comes only to a few fortunate and fully prepared students—and the fruit is auspicious and blissful.

At this stage we study and practice with determination and understanding. We start getting a taste of self-discipline, self-study, and practice. The ego becomes purer. It realizes the joy that manifests from the union of the little ego with the higher Self. Thus, without any formal instruction, the ego is drawn to the idea of surrender—the natural urge to become part of the

Great One by losing the little one.

Our longing to fill the empty space in the cave of the heart grows. We feel the strong need for silent communication from an enlightened, compassionate heart to our heart. We look toward someone who has gained that experience, a master who has heard the whisper of divine love and is capable of whispering into the depths of our heart without making a sound, and finally we are able to trust him. We are ready to pay any price for that soundless whisper. Someone deep within tells us that if we can receive the whisper of divine love, even at the cost of losing all else, it's still a good bargain.

The more this longing grows, the clearer our vision becomes; the clearer our vision, the firmer our conviction. The delight springing forth from our practice motivates us to do more practice. We become a true disciple—a vessel of discipline—and consequently the master appears in his true form. We post no more "no trespassing" signs as we did in the beginning. Our reservations disappear as our ego realizes that those who love and care for us pose no threat. We become a lover of *satsanga*, the company of the teacher and other wise ones. Neither teacher nor student is a guest or host any longer—they are part of each other. The idea that "this is mine" and "that is yours" loses its binding power and is replaced by a new understanding: "what is mine is yours." At this stage the spiritual bond has attained its sublime state—totally unconditional and grounded in pure love, understanding, fearlessness, and firm conviction.

THE TEACHER WITHIN

Regardless of whether we are beginning, intermediate, or advanced seekers, we undertake our quest only if we are inspired from within. Then, propelled by the inner force of self-inspiration and self-motivation, we search for clearer and more definitive guidance. This inner force is called *atma shakti*, the power of the soul. It is the teacher within. It dispels negativity such as sloth, complacency, and skepticism, as well as lack of courage and enthusiasm. Without it, no one can ever gather the courage to leave the confines of worldly circumstances and the limiting conditions of the mind.

The teacher within is ever vigilant, sending its inspiration from the depths of our being. When we listen and comply, we receive *atma kripa* (the grace of oneself). If *atma kripa* flows freely, without obstruction, we can obtain the highest illumination without help from any other source. When the horizon of our inner consciousness is darkened by mental confusion, however, we fail to be fully receptive to the grace of the Self, so only a fragment of it touches our being. Even this touch allows us to sense that the totality of the truth is within our reach, and that we must realize it. This impels us to find the external teacher who can teach us the method for unfolding the teacher within.

The external teacher knows we are so estranged from our inner world that an immediate introduction to the inner Self would be fruitless. We have been partially blessed with the grace of our inner Self, however, so the external teacher also knows it is of the utmost importance to help us receive the other three forms of grace: the grace of the scriptures, the grace of God, and the grace of the guru. The spiritual journey gathers momentum only when all four forms of grace have been fully united.

Thus an experienced teacher who has undergone arduous training himself, under the guidance of a competent master, skillfully introduces us to the wisdom of the scriptures, which have been verified generation after generation for untold ages. When we study the scriptures by ourselves we may understand them partially, but when we study these same scriptures under the guidance of a teacher we gain insight into their deeper meaning, and are guided by it. This is *shastra kripa* (the grace of the scriptures).

When we practice the teachings of those scriptures, however, we do not always find their promises fulfilled. Furthermore, we encounter difficulties in practicing the teachings, and the scriptures do not tell us how to overcome them. Although the teacher stresses the value of scriptural knowledge, and the importance of using the spiritual map which has been so accurately drawn by previous travelers, he also points out the shortcomings of book-learning, reminding us of the currents and crosscurrents that undermine the efficacy of self-effort. To help us overcome these invisible obstacles the teacher shows us the way to receive *Ishvara kripa* (the grace of God). He guides us in such a way that the stream of spirituality is mingled with love and devotion for higher Truth. The more love and devotion grow in our heart, the more prepared we are for receiving and retaining the grace of God. The more powerful the current of divine grace, the greater the inner purification. The more purified the heart, the more fertile the soil. The more fertile the soil, the faster the seed of faith sprouts and grows. Once it takes root in our heart, spirituality blossoms.

When we begin receiving both the grace of the scriptures and the grace of God, the teacher sees that his investment is multiplying. He experiences a delightful urge to give the student more and more. This is the fourth grace, *guru kripa* (the grace of the guru). And once this process begins, one form of grace continually invites the other forms of grace into our life. This is all because the teacher within us—our own *atma shakti*—has led us to the teacher without, and the teacher without has lovingly introduced us to the teacher within.

Ceaseless awareness of so'ham is the luminous flame in the lamp of meditation. In the blissful light of Self-realization radiating from this flame, delusion rooted in dualism— the cause of bondage—is forever annihilated.

Ramcharit Manas,
Uttar Khanda 118

CHAPTER 4

THE UNIVERSAL MANTRA

The yearning of the student and the compassion of the teacher are like two poles of a magnet—each is attracted to and drawn by the other. The teacher, however, is impelled by a stronger force than is the student, for the desire to find a student manifests the compassion of the Primordial Master, whose perennial task is to search for students and transport them from darkness into the realm of Light. This Primordial Master is none other than God, the Supreme Being from whom the stream of knowledge flows eternally. According to the *Yoga Sutra*, the Primordial Master is free from karmas and the fruits of karmas, and is omniscient, omnipresent, and omnipotent. The Primordial Master is the teacher of all previous teachers and the soul of all living beings.

The knowledge and compassion of the Primordial Master manifesting in a human being makes that person a teacher. Driven by pure compassion, a true teacher interacts with his students on behalf of the Primordial Master. Thus, the Primordial Master, using the teacher as an instrument, collects lamp, wick, oil, and matches, and lights the lamp for those who are stranded in darkness. Under the guidance of the Primordial Master, seekers and teachers move toward each other. Fully awakened teachers are aware that the Primordial Master is constantly guiding them, but most teachers are only half-awake and do not experience this guidance consciously, even though they too are working on Its behalf.

The Primordial Master, either in the form of the inner teacher (inner inspiration and self-motivation) or in the form of external teachers, journeys through the dark night of the soul in search of those who have fallen asleep, and gently awakens them. This is the first step in initiation.

We don't usually notice this first step, because our ego comes forward and says to us, "Aha, it's me who is inspired." No matter. The purpose of this subtle but most significant of initiations is to stir us to shake off our lifelong slumber. After this invisible initiation has taken effect, our attention begins to turn from worldly affairs to spirituality. The grace of God follows. It comes in many forms: we get fed up with the world; or the world gets fed up with us; or we go to Hawaii to celebrate a big promotion, and end up reading this book on mantra and initiation instead; or we notice that we're aging, and begin to wonder if we have made the best use of our lives. In ways myriad and mysterious, the omniscient, compassionate Master guides us until we finally realize that we are seekers. Lamp, wick, oil, and matches are coming together, but we notice only when the lamp is lit.

This level of initiation takes place when we have already learned the basic principles of spirituality, the most fundamental of which is that we have put ourselves in bondage, and that no one else can give us freedom. The inner chamber of our heart has become dark through our own actions; it cannot be illumined by another's efforts. Other travelers can point the way according to their knowledge and experience, but ultimately we must walk the path if we are to attain the goal. This understanding dawns only after the Primordial Master has mysteriously initiated us.

Once we have gained this level of understanding, we eventually find an instructor and learn the technique of the inward journey: how to keep the lamp burning steadily by trimming the wick and replenishing the oil. We learn how to maintain a steady practice, how to keep from becoming disheartened when we pass through rough periods, and how to revitalize our practice before we become discouraged and drop it. That we continue our practice with ever-increasing interest is one of the sure signs that we have met the right teacher and have been introduced to the right technique of spiritual practice.

When teacher and student live in one another's company, it becomes the teacher's duty to protect the student from doubt, carelessness, laziness, and procrastination. This is protecting the flame. Because we are working with a teacher, our growing interest in our practice and the gradual attenuation of our bad habits unfold spontaneously. But practically speaking, some effort on our part is required to overcome our lifelong and intense involvement in the external world. We need to deliberately cut back on our worldly concerns to make time for spiritual concerns, for if we are not careful, the world consumes us.

Working, sleeping, eating, shopping, bathing, dressing, socializing, and attending to family affairs leave us little time and energy for directing our attention toward our true source.

The art of living in the world can, however, be mastered without ignoring the supreme goal of life. When we achieve this mastery while retaining our spiritual focus, we achieve a state of balance and harmony, disregarding neither worldly obligations nor spiritual needs. To meet this challenge, we must adopt a very practical approach to spiritual practice, utilizing the body, breath, and mind, which are its tools. If one of these tools is missing or defective, or if there is no coordination among them, we cannot expect to practice successfully, no matter how good the mantra or how great the teacher.

A stiff, tired body, an erratic habit of breathing, and a scattered mind are not fit for mantra meditation, but correcting these conditions requires systematic effort. We can make the body strong, healthy, and flexible by practicing gentle yoga exercises called *asanas*. By learning to sit in a comfortable, relaxed, and steady posture, with our head, neck, and trunk aligned, we allow *prana* (energy) to flow freely throughout the body. We can increase our energy, and bring harmony to the functioning of the pranic forces, by cultivating the habit of breathing smoothly and diaphragmatically, without jerks or noise, and without pauses between the inhalation and exhalation. Finally, we can learn how to eliminate distractions by practicing *pratyahara* (the technique of sense withdrawal), beginning with the practice of systematic relaxation techniques. Appendix A, "Preparation for Mantra Initiation," includes basic instructions in these techniques, which lay the foundation for the higher practices of mantra meditation. This is a balanced program, and by following it we can energize our tired body, calm our erratic breath, develop an inner focus, and learn how to bring harmony to our scattered mind.

THE RHYTHM OF LIFE

After we have begun to gain some proficiency with these techniques, we must next give the mind an object to hold on to so that it may become free of distractions. At this early stage the best object is the natural sound of the breath—the sound *so'ham* (pronounced "so hum"). This is a mantra in its own right. It comes from the Upanishads, and it is practiced by students of both the Yoga and Vedanta traditions. Yogis emphasize meditation, and so they practice this mantra differently from the followers of Vedanta, who emphasize self-analysis and contemplative techniques. Before discussing these differences, however, let us explore the nature of the sound itself.

So'ham is the mantric manifestation of the vital energy of all living beings because it is the natural sound of the breath. Breathing connects us all with the cosmic life-force—through inhalation we receive a constant supply of vital energy, and through exhalation we release that which is not needed in our system. As long as this process goes on, we stay alive. When it stops, we die.

According to the yogis, breathing is totally dependent on the sound *so'ham*. They hold that this sound precedes even the first breath; it is in response to this sound that the psyche instinctively commands the brain and the nervous system to start breathing the moment we emerge from the womb.

Day and night the sound *so'ham* reverberates as we inhale and exhale. Erratic breathing and a noisy mind render this sound inaudible to us, however, because it is subtler than the breathing process. To experience it, sit in a quiet place and focus on your breath. If your breath is tranquil, and if you have eliminated any noise and jerkiness in your breathing, you will hear the sound *sooo* in the inhalation and *hammmmm* in the exhalation. After a time you will feel as though someone inside you is constantly saying *sooohammm* in each breath. This is the rhythm of life.

Personality, speech, emotions, and the sense of attraction or repulsion are a few of the ways in which the life-force radiates from us. We also radiate different degrees and shades of light, sound, electricity, magnetism, and gravitational energy. Every cell of the body has its own vibratory pattern, and, based on this pattern, sound waves emerge from each cell. But all the cells in an organism must function in a coordinated manner; they must all vibrate within a specific spectrum, which is defined by the subtle energy of the sound *so'ham*—the collective sound of all the cells of the body. Furthermore, by imbuing the cells with this sound, heard at a particular pace and in a particular rhythm, Mother Nature coordinates the vibratory pattern of all the cells of a particular species. The pace and rhythm determines how rapidly or slowly a particular creature should breathe; in turn, the breathing pattern regulates the metabolic activity of the body.

From this standpoint, Mother Nature is the first guru of all living beings. She initiates us into the sacred sound of *so'ham,* and thus we begin the journey of life. By planting this mantra in the depths of our being, she establishes law and order so that we may live and grow harmoniously. Through the power of this mantra we are connected to and in harmony with the cosmos. In the scriptures, the presiding force of this mantra is called *sutratma* (the thread atma); it is also known as *pranatma,* the thread of life.

Each time we encounter an unwholesome and distressing experience we disturb the pace and rhythm of the breath that has been established by nature. Such disturbances occur throughout our life, breaking the harmony between our breath and the natural sound of *so'ham.* This in turn disrupts the current of the life-force. Reestablishing a natural and proper breathing pattern, by allowing the breath to follow the sound *so'ham,* restores this harmony.

Attending to the sound *so'ham,* then, is attending to the rhythm of life. But because this sound is subtler than the breath, we must begin by paying attention to the breath. For only when the breath has become quiet, smooth, and tranquil, and the mind steady, can we attend to *so'ham.* By introducing the mind to this sound, we are introducing it to the perennial life-force that first set the body-mind organism in motion, allowing it to touch the source of *prana shakti* (vital energy). Then, by allowing mind, breath, and *so'ham* to flow together as one integral stream, we create harmony at various levels of our personality. Peace dawns. The mind no longer looks for excuses to run into the external world (at least not for a while). This is the intrinsic characteristic of *so'ham;* this is why it is the universal mantra, and why there is no need for a human teacher to formally initiate us into its use. If we pay attention to the breath, we will find that the mantra is already there.

THE MEANING OF *SO'HAM*

So'ham is first mentioned in the Upanishads, ancient texts written in Sanskrit, and in that language *so'ham* means "I am That." However, as we have seen, all mantras belong to the universal language, and Sanskrit is not this language. Sanskrit is unique only in the sense that, for the most part, it has come to us through revelation. Its phonemes, words, and groups of words were revealed to the seers in their deep *samadhi,* and eventually they were compiled in the form of the Vedas. *So'ham* means "I am That," however, not because Sanskrit dictionaries say so, but because this meaning was revealed to the seers simultaneously with the sound. Let's explore how this came about.

Deep in *samadhi* a sage in ancient times was immersed in the unitary state of consciousness, totally one with the Absolute. When he descended from that state he experienced his self-existence in relation to the experience of the Absolute and, as he did so, the essence of duality emerged. Because he remembered his experience of unity, the sage was still in a state of deep tranquility, but he was separate now, and he wondered how it was possible to be both at one with, and totally separate from, the universal being. Then, as he breathed, he felt the link that connected the individual and the universal. He heard the sound *so 'ham*. With the sound *so* he was inhaling; with the sound *ham* he was exhaling. As he inhaled, he experienced the Universal Being walking in and realized that it is He who enters this body with the breath, bringing freshness and vitality to the individual trapped there. In the form of the sound *so* waves of divinity and immortality enter and rejuvenate the individual. This thrilling experience spontaneously unfolded the knowledge that the sound *so* meant "That"—the Immortal Being.

This realization simultaneously led him to experience the other component of this truth: I exist because of That; I am because of That. This experience was even more vivid when he noticed that the sound *so* with his inhalation immediately merged into the sound *ham* as he exhaled—and with this sound *ham* the sage felt himself merging into the cosmos. So for him, the sound *ham* meant "I." As this process continued, his experience was: I am That, That I am, I am That, That I am . . .

The next thing the seer discovered is that if he inhaled without anticipating the oncoming exhalation, the sound of the inhalation was a flat *sah* with a little aspirate sound at the end. The sound of inhalation is heard as *so* only if the exhalation follows immediately. The sage also realized that if exhalation is not preceded by inhalation, the sound *aham* appears in the outgoing breath. Thus, if inhalation and exhalation are disconnected from each other, they contain two distinct sounds—*sah* and *aham*—but the moment the breath flows without interruption or pause, each merging into the other,

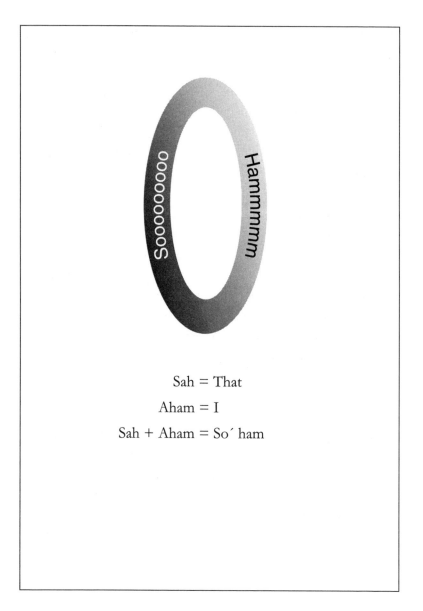

Sah = That

Aham = I

Sah + Aham = So´ ham

Figure 1

and each emerging from the other, the sounds *sah* and *aham* turn into *so'ham*. From this realization arose one of the grammatical rules of Sanskrit: an aspirate sound preceded by *a* and followed by *a* turns into *o*. Experiments have shown that it is impossible to pronounce *sah aham* without creating a pause between inhalation and exhalation and without disrupting the normal heart beat. However, no pause is created by listening to the sound *so'ham* and letting the breath follow it.

Even in ancient times, *so'ham* was held sacred, for both meditative and contemplative purposes, by philosophers and spiritual seekers following different paths. In the Upanishads, for example, this mantra is one of the *maha vakyas* (great utterances). In other traditions, philosophers and spiritual seekers have all accepted *so'ham* as a means of self-analysis and contemplation. The meaning "I am That" is at once so concise and so general that it can be used within the context of any philosophical or religious doctrine. For example, it can be interpreted to mean: Essentially I am that Divine Being who enters me, sustains me, embraces me, and eventually leads me to Its immortal abode. Or it can mean: I am part of that Cosmic Being who sustains my life and guides me through life's journey. Or: I am a devotee of that Supreme One, and He is my Lord. This flexibility is one of the reasons this mantra is universal.

MEDITATION ON *SO'HAM*

Because everyone is born with it, there is no need for a formal initiation into this mantra. However, because the Vedantic tradition emphasizes contemplation and self-analysis, that student does need formal training in the specific subtradition of Vedanta to which she belongs. Contemplation based on the sound *so'ham* is a very precise and systematic practice, but it can yield a complete result only under the guidance of a competent master. If we are using this mantra only as an object for concentration, however, all we need to know is the proper technique for focusing on it: sitting with the head, neck, and trunk straight; breathing without noise, jerks, and pauses; and listening to the sound *so'ham* deep in the breath.

This technique induces a state of tranquility and restfulness, for listening to the sound *so'ham* as we breathe requires us to quiet ourselves and focus our awareness inward, transcending external noise, and withdrawing our scattered mind from worldly objects. The moment we resolve to listen to the sound in each breath, we automatically gather the forces of mind that have been scattered and diffused by the external world, and summon them to flow inward. Then we are aware of the rhythmic vibration of the mantra. Thus, by gently maneuvering the mind to come in touch with the sound *so'ham*, we help it to disentangle itself from the trivial concerns of worldly affairs which uselessly drain our energies. This gives the mind a chance to rest, and in this state our senses, nervous system, and all the organs and limbs of the body drink the elixir of life.

The mind has formed the habit of running into the external world, incessantly contacting one object after another. It craves change; it becomes bored when asked to stay in one place for too long. For this reason, while meditating on the sound *so'ham* is very rewarding for a month or two, two problems soon emerge which compel us to find a more specific and powerful tool to lead the mind through the maze of its distractions.

The first problem results from the fact that in the beginning we had general and recognizable concerns. The stress we create in our daily life and store at the surface level of our personality is washed off by the simple techniques of relaxation, breathing, and meditation on the sound *so'ham*. This helps us to overcome fatigue and exhaustion, recharging our nervous system and ridding ourselves of the stress freshly stored in the conscious mind. Removing these short-term problems floating at the outer layer of our being has an immediate and noticeable effect. That's why, for the first few months, meditating on *so'ham* yields remarkable results.

But once our nervous system is relatively balanced and the conscious mind is calmer, we begin to notice more potent unconscious issues coming forward. Now, instead of tension in the body and irregularities in the breath, powerful anxieties and unconscious memories disturb our peace. Meditation on the *so'ham* mantra does not work very well to quiet these.

So'ham is a mantra of the fundamental life-force, *prana*. It pulls together all the pieces of our mind, senses, and body, removing our scatteredness, bringing a sense of wholeness, and most important, quieting our mind. But once this has happened, this quieter and more concentrated mind tells us that there are deeper and more subtle problems beneath the surface. The meditative mind does not create these problems; it simply reveals them: the hidden facets in our personality that must be faced and conquered. For an under-informed and impatient meditator, this poses a problem.

The second problem is boredom. To a mind that has adjusted itself to the rush and roar, pains and pleasures, and ups and downs of worldly life, watching the breath and listening to *so'ham* every day for months and months eventually becomes dull. So this mind summons its crafty skills and comes up with countless ways of creating the excitement it craves. It is doubly anxious to do this because it does not want unconscious material to surface. So it deliberately creates distractions.

At this stage there is no point in fighting with the mind. The material beneath the surface is quite substantial, and we must find a way to deal with it. We must get in touch with a higher force, from which we can draw the inner strength and power of determination that will enable us to illuminate the unlit corners of the unconscious mind, where the ghosts of our *samskaras* (the subtle impressions of our previous actions) dwell. Now, even though we experience the thread of the life-force running through the fabric of our being, it is not enough. We need a more powerful tool to make our mind truly one-pointed, a tool that will purify our heart and heighten our self-awareness. *So'ham* has prepared us for this next level of practice: it is time for formal initiation into a guru mantra.

And when he came up out of the
water, immediately he saw the
heavens opened and the Spirit
descending upon him like a dove;
and a voice came from heaven,
" Thou art my beloved Son; with
thee I am well pleased."

Mark 1:10-11

THE POWER OF INITIATION

From a spiritual perspective, the object of meditation is more important than the process. If developing concentration were the only goal of meditation, we could focus our mind on any attractive object. Yogic literature is full of stories about meditators who gained enormous powers of concentration either by practicing *trataka* (fixed gazing) or by focusing their mind on an object of their own choosing. Yet these meditators were not transformed. They remained prey to ignorance and all the pains and miseries that it spawns: egoism, attachment, aversion, and fear. But since our goal is the source of consciousness, we must meditate on an object that is connected with it intrinsically so that it will lead our mind there.

There is no meditation without concentration. For this a one-pointed mind is important, but determining the direction that our concentrated mind will travel is even more important. The quality of the object of concentration is what purifies our awareness and enables it to penetrate the various layers of our inner being. No matter how attractive and captivating an object is, it cannot bring about spiritual unfoldment unless spiritual wisdom is its inherent quality. A true mantra is such an object.

The power of a mantra lies in its ability to lead the meditator to the same state of consciousness attained by the seer who first experienced the mantra. The seed of divine revelation is planted in the heart of the student during initiation, but time is required for that seed to sprout, grow, flower, and give fruit. Just as the fertility of the soil and weather conditions determine how fast a physical seed will grow into a plant, so the purity of the initiate's mind and body determines how long it will take for the mantra to reveal its power. But this much is certain: sooner or later the seed will blossom and produce inner illumination.

According to the scriptures the true form of a mantra is not what we see when it is written or what we hear when it is articulated. Rather, the essence of a mantra is *nada* (pure, unstruck, eternal sound), what the evangelist John was referring to when he wrote, "In the beginning was the Word, and the Word was with God, and the Word was God." *Nada* contains the entire universe in its unmanifest form. It is the source of all mantras, and it is their true form.

Initiation kindles the light of the divine sound in the aspirant's mind and heart, and thus dispels the darkness of ignorance. During initiation the teacher utters a mantra in its articulate form, and the initiate hears it, but even so it is essentially a manifestation of *nada*. As we practice according to the instructions given us at the time of initiation, the pronunciation of the mantra is refined—first we repeat it mentally, then we begin to hear it. As our practice deepens, the sound of the mantra becomes more subtle and silent, until eventually we neither repeat nor hear it, but rejoice inwardly in its soundless sound. This is the most pristine state of the mantra, one that duplicates the original experience of the mantra's first seer.

INITIATION OUTWEIGHS BOOK-LEARNING

Just as every religion has its own name and form for God, which it considers to be superior to all others, so do most mantric and Tantric scriptures consider their own particular mantra to be superior to all others. This situation can be found even within a single text—every chapter proclaims the supremacy of whatever mantra or yantra is being discussed. There are thousands of mantras, and there are thousands of texts, and thousands of chapters within texts, each extolling the virtues of its own particular mantra. So how do we determine which of these is the most suitable for us?

According to the adepts of mantra science, mantras described in books are like a menu in a restaurant. The menu gives us an idea of what to expect, but if we are to eat, the order has to be placed and the food served. Similarly, knowing about a mantra is entirely different from receiving one. The first depends on study, the second on initiation, and if we rely on study to select a mantra we will run into problems.

The first problem is that the scriptures related to mantra science are written in Sanskrit. Even the mantras of the Jaina and Buddhist schools either are directly derived from Sanskrit sources or they have been slightly modified and rendered in

Prakrit, Pali, Tibetan, Chinese, or Japanese. If we could read the original scriptures we would find that most mantras—especially the spiritually elevating meditative mantras—are written in code, making it impossible for us to understand them. And decoding these verses in order to get the mantra in its correct form is a science in itself, one that is taught only directly by the teacher to her initiate student. It is true that some texts do explain the basic mantric codes, but none provides enough detail to enable a reader not instructed by the oral tradition to arrive at the correct form of the mantra.

Another problem is doubt. Let us assume we have mastered Sanskrit, and after a long period of study and intellectual analysis we have selected a mantra from a book to practice. We will meditate on that mantra only as long as we have faith in it, and because we have chosen it ourselves a part of our mind will question whether it is the right mantra for us. As the waves of doubt become stronger, our faith in this self-chosen mantra will erode. Then, if we continue studying, we will come across other texts that stress the importance of practicing other mantras, and faith in the mantra we have selected by ourselves will dwindle further. Eventually we will abandon it for another. Pandits (spiritually inspired Sanskrit scholars) often fall into this trap. They repeatedly select mantras from books, practicing one for a while, then dropping it for another. At least they are selecting mantras from original sources, not from secondary texts whose authenticity is questionable to begin with (a practice that has become epidemic in the New Age culture).

But even if we master both Sanskrit and the science of decoding mantras, manage to find a mantra in its correct form, and do not lose faith in it, a final obstacle remains. Realizing that aspirants who have not attained purity of heart or gained control over their mind and senses are likely to misuse the mantra *shakti,* the original seers of the mantras or other sages in the lineage have imposed certain rules and laws that must be followed in order to unveil the power of a mantra that we practice without receiving it through initiation. As described in the scriptures, these laws include knowledge of the relationship between the mantra and its seer, as well as knowledge of the meter, of the presiding deity, of the syllable in which the *bija* (seed) resides, of the syllable in which the *shakti* (the kinetic power of the mantra) resides, and most important, of the syllable in which the *kilaka* (the mantra's anchoring effect) lies. In other words, unveiling the power of such a mantra requires knowing its six limbs *(sad anga):* seer, meter, presiding deity, seed, kinetic power, and anchor.

To understand this better, let us take the six-syllable mantra of the Divine Mother—the *navarna* mantra—as an example. The seers of this mantra are Brahma, Vishnu, Rudra, and Gayatri. The meter is a combination of *ushnik* and *anushtup.* Kali, Lakshmi, and Sarasvati rule over the power of the mantra. *Aim* is the seed; *hrim* is the kinetic power; and *klim* is the anchor. In the practice of highly potent mantras such as this it is also important to know the technique for synchronizing the forces of these six limbs with different energies in the body, a process known as *nyasa.* This entails synchronizing our own physiological and biological energies with the forces of our psyche, thus enabling us to attune our entire being to the mantra.

Knowledge of the seer creates a link with that seer. The more we know about the first seer and subsequent adepts who have practiced the mantra, the more faith in and devotion for the self-chosen mantra grows in our heart. During the practice we feel connected to them and that brings a great sense of joy to our meditation. The realization that we are not alone, but are guided and accompanied by those compassionate ones, is a source of security and fearlessness. Similarly, knowing the meter, *shakti,* deity, seed, and anchor engenders self-confidence and trust in the practice we have undertaken.

Except for some popular mantras such as *gayatri,* however, the only instructions found in the scriptures for all six mantric limbs and the auxiliary practices that accompany them are incomplete and unclear. Thus, practicing without being initiated and without proper guidance may bring doubt and dissatisfaction as its fruit.

THE POWER OF AN AWAKENED MANTRA

In an unbroken spiritual lineage, the wisdom of mantra flows incessantly from teacher to student in all of its purity and fullness. Through initiation a teacher not only imparts the mantra and the correct method of practicing it, but also sows the seed of spiritual wisdom directly in the heart of the student. A teacher may have knowledge of many scriptures and their mantra practices, but she imparts only those that she herself has received from her lineage.

Mantras received from the lineage are called *jagrata* (awakened) mantras, and only they have the power to engender an awakening in the student. We might find a mantra that is written correctly in a book, and begin practicing it with all the proper steps, but still fail to receive the promised result. But when an accomplished master confers the same mantra, it exhibits its powers. As an example, I will share one of my own experiences.

When I first came to the United States, I was fascinated with one of the most revered scriptures, *Saundaryalahari*. It consists of a hundred mantras, and it is the subject of a number of well-known commentaries—one of which explains the practical application of the mantras. According to that commentary the aspirant must repeat the mantra (in this case a long verse composed in a melodious meter) one thousand times every day for forty-five days. My master, Sri Swami Rama, was in a distant city, so I undertook the practice on my own and completed it. But to my disappointment I did not notice any of the effects the commentary described.

I thought that perhaps my mind was not one-pointed, or my heart not pure enough. Or perhaps my karmas were not in my favor. I also remembered a saint saying that in the Kali Yuga (this present era in which our morality, inner strength, and power of determination have declined) these practices have to be done four times more intensely than the scriptures stipulate. Thus, I continued the practice and exceeded even that amount. Still the promised result did not manifest.

Meanwhile, my master called me to him. One day he said

very lovingly, "I want you to do a special practice. It is very important for you." Pointing at a book he said, "Can you bring that book?"

I got up and brought the book to him. It was the *Saundaryalahari*, the scripture I had been studying and practicing on my own. Swamiji opened the book to the verse I had repeated thousands of times, and putting his finger on it said, "Practice this mantra for thirty-three days."

I asked, "Is there any ritual or anything else to be done as a part of this practice?"

"No. Just do *japa* [the repetition of mantra]."

"How many times, Swamiji?"

"Thirty-three times every day."

Because I had already repeated that same mantra a thousand times every day for several months with no discernible effect, a subtle but potentially destructive thought came in my mind: If nothing happened when I repeated the mantra a thousand times, then what could I expect from thirty-three repetitions? Trying to hide my ego and doubt under the guise of false innocence, I said, "Only thirty-three times, Swamiji?"

"You can do it forty-five times if you want," he replied.

Still I argued: "Just forty-five times? Is it enough?"

Very lovingly, Swamiji looked at me and said, "If you really want, you can repeat it a hundred times a day."

So I did the practice, and the result was as fulfilling and delightful as the text had described. With a sense of deep gratitude, I went to Swamiji and reported that, through his blessings, I had completed the practice with a wonderful result. To my dismay Swamiji did not seem happy with me. After a couple of minutes of silence, he said gently, "My master has done these *sadhanas* and simplified them for the students. Now people instructed by you will have to repeat this mantra not less than a hundred times." I got the lesson.

The adepts keep the mantras particular to their lineage awakened. Mantras that are safeguarded by the lineage are like gunpowder: a master adds a spark, and they burst into flames. But mantras that are disconnected from the lineage are like soggy logs: a huge amount of burning coal is required to make them catch fire, and before they do they produce a lot of smoke. A master understands the value of an awakened mantra. She plants it in the seeker's heart, igniting it only when she knows that all conditions are favorable—even the best medicine should be given only in the proper dose. As the great tenth-century yogi Guru Gorakh Nath said:

> It is important for a teacher to utter a word very carefully. He must give that which a student can contain. If he forcefully transmits more than can fit in the container, the container will rupture. If he carelessly tosses it in the container, a good part of it will spill, and that is a waste.
>
> The disciple asks: The content is big and the container is small. Tell me how to solve this problem, O Master.
>
> The master says: When it is imparted in its natural course, and is received in a natural manner, there an ever-growing interest naturally unfolds. As interest is transformed into longing and love, the container begins to

grow. This will make the master spontaneously place the amount of wealth in that container that matches the size of the container.

Gorakh Bani, verses 254-56

INITIATION

Mantra initiation is a process, not a one-time event. In the scriptures it is called *krama diksha*. Often a teacher gives a *bija* mantra (a seed syllable) as the first step. Then as the student practices, the teacher will impart additional *bija* mantras, or a specific mantra central to her particular lineage.

In addition to providing a definite direction and a suitable vehicle for the inward journey, initiation is a way of establishing the intimate relationship between student and teacher so necessary to the ongoing process of spiritual unfoldment. Mantra initiation is a big commitment on the part of both teacher and student. As students, each of us must overcome our skepticism and doubt before committing ourselves to this auspicious undertaking. We must watch our natural inclinations, and we must study the intensity of our spiritual yearning to know when it is appropriate to request a mantra.

Mantra initiation is not a contract—there is nothing like making an agreement to impart or receive a mantra. Instead, as we have seen in the two preceding chapters, an indiscernible process of moving toward mantra initiation begins long before we meet our spiritual guide and request personal guidance. In this age of science and technology most of us are drawn to meditation because it is scientifically valid. Its health and psy-

chological benefits are self-evident, and in this respect meditation is a technique to gain rest for the body and peace of mind.

But after meditating awhile we notice the shortcomings in
these preliminary techniques. At some point we get tired of a
meditation practice that is still a kind of mental exercise. We
feel that we have reached a plateau in our meditative relaxation.
We want to experience the reality that transcends body, breath,
and mind—and a desire awakens in us to go beyond the limits
of science and gain an experience that cannot be induced by
mere techniques. We long to experience the mystical dimension
of meditation. This is the doorway to spiritual advancement.

On the teacher's side, a deep feeling of love and desire to
give the best of herself to the student spontaneously unfolds.
She feels an urge to share the blessing that has illuminated her
own life, and this unconditional love generates the courage to
accept a disciple even though there may be convincing intellectual arguments against doing so. The teacher feels a powerful wave of compassion urging her to accept the student as an
inseparable part of her own life, without caring about the student's merits and demerits. And as the heart of the teacher
opens in this way, the student feels the urge to surrender to the
Divine. This process is spontaneous; it takes place without
planning on either side.

Although the flow of compassion is the medium through
which the guru mantra (the mantra that we receive during initiation) descends, this is always accompanied by *prajna,* the
intuitive wisdom described in chapter 2. At the time of initiation the teacher is accompanied, guided, and protected by the

masters of the lineage. There is no way such a teacher can slip from the ground of discrimination and become sentimental. A teacher has neither the choice nor the power to give that which is not supposed to be given. But remember, a spiritual teacher—a mantra initiator—is she who is appointed by a qualified teacher belonging to an unbroken guru-disciple lineage. Only a self-proclaimed initiator, or an initiator appointed by a fake guru, someone who has not become an integral part of the ever-flowing stream of knowledge, can make a mistake—because such a teacher's knowledge is based on mere book-learning.

During the time of initiation a genuine teacher is nonexistent as a person. She is simply an instrument of the tradition. Compelled by compassion (*karuna* or *anugraha shakti*), wisdom (*prajna*) comes forth in the form of mantra *shakti,* and the specific mantra appropriate for the student being initiated springs forth from the pool of the lineage. A teacher who has lost her individuality in the master can never impart less or more than what has been willed by the master.

THE *BIJA* MANTRA

Although this is not a strict rule, the first mantra a teacher imparts is generally a preparatory mantra—a *bija* (or seed) mantra. Although divine protection and guidance are general characteristics of all seed mantras, each has its own specific transformative power. They are the omnipresent representatives of nature's finest forces, not only within the individual but also within the cosmos. In their anthropomorphic forms these forces are deities—gods and goddesses—and *bija* mantras are their sound forms. We comprehend their mantric forms when we have "ears to hear," and envision their anthropomorphic forms when we have "eyes to see."

Sounds waves in the form of words have no meaning in and of themselves. Meaning results when a speaker and a hearer are at the same level of understanding. In the case of seed mantras, however, their meaning is revealed to the seers. Later, through *sankalpa shakti* (the power of will and determination), the seers allow the meaning to flow inseparably with the sound waves. Regardless of the hearer's level of comprehension, these seed mantras illuminate their meanings because their potentiality has been awakened by the power of that first seer.

Most *bija* mantras consist of just one syllable, but there are some that consist of two or more syllables, or are formed by a combination of several seed mantras. *Bija* mantras composed of several syllables are extremely difficult for the tongue to pronounce or the ear to hear. Because the scriptures related to these mantras are in the Sanskrit language, the mantras are written in Indian scripts (such as Devanagari, Tamil, and Bengali). *Bija* mantras are the vehicles of sound, not meaning. Sanskrit letters and Indian scripts are used simply to crystallize the vibratory patterns of those sounds and to represent them in a manner that we can understand.

Seed mantras contain the potential of the Divine to manifest into the grand tree of spiritual illumination. They are like engines pulling a train, and for this reason they are often called *shakti* mantras. They are given for the purpose of preparing the solid foundation on which the teacher later builds the whole structure of spirituality.

CONFUSION AND BOOKS

These days there is much confusion about *bija* mantras because some of the scriptures on mantra *sadhana* have been translated into modern languages, and we are now able to read fascinating interpretations of them. Some modern writers have even catalogued these mantras, without having acquired sufficient knowledge and experiential insight. Today books written in Hindi, Bengali, Marathi, Gujarati, and English contain charts of the *bija* mantras and instructions on how to use them for different purposes. Unfortunately, the authors of such books are only magnifying their ignorance by creating the false impression that selecting a mantra is a matter for intellectual analysis. What is more, they frequently distort the meaning and purpose of a mantra by failing to understand that the scriptures have deliberately made exaggerated claims about it—for very good reasons.

Om is a case in point. One of the most popular sacred sounds, Om is the seed mantra of universal consciousness. It has been expounded in the Vedas, the Upanishads, and throughout Tantric literature. Independent texts have been written solely to explain its profound meaning. Om has even been used as a vehicle for elaborating philosophical and metaphysical doctrines.

For example, according to the *Mandukya Upanishad* the

three basic constituent sounds of Om are *a, u,* and *m;* the third syllable *m* is followed by the sound of silence. These three syllables represent the three levels of reality corresponding to our waking, dreaming, and sleeping states; the silence that follows represents transcendental reality. While expounding this doctrine, the *Mandukya Upanishad* explains how the whole world evolves from Om and merges with Om, and how by meditating on Om we can gain access to all three states of consciousness—as well as the fourth: transcendental Truth. The commentators on this Upanishad elaborate the doctrine to the point that the reader begins to feel that Om is the only mantra worth practicing. Yet if we read the scriptures that expound on the *gayatri* mantra, we have the same reaction.

According to Vedic and Upanishadic texts, the *gayatri* mantra is the mother of the Vedas. All the mantras of the Vedas are said to come from *gayatri.* The whole universe evolves from *gayatri,* exists in *gayatri,* and at the time of dissolution, merges in *gayatri.* Just as the three syllables of Om are representative of (and according to some scriptures identical with) the states of waking, dreaming, and deep sleep, the three parts of *gayatri* represent these same three states of consciousness. The fourth, which represents transcendent Truth, is known only to the knowers of Brahman. The scriptures also tell us that the *gayatri* mantra and Om are virtually identical. What does this mean?

Mimamsa, a highly respected school of Vedic philosophy, provides the most profound discussions of the science of studying mantras and understanding their meanings, but unfortunately is the school least known among scholars and spiritual seekers. The texts of Mimamsa explain that the scriptures make exaggerated claims about a certain mantra, or the practice related to it, in order to engender faith and create a devotional environment—thus inspiring their followers to pursue the practice wholeheartedly.

During Muslim rule (from the ninth through the seventeenth centuries A.D.) the literacy rate in India declined. The intent behind these scriptural claims was forgotten, and they began to be taken literally. Because scriptures in written form were rare, and because only a few of those who possessed them knew how to read, most people were dependent on oral exposition. The blind began leading the blind. Under these circumstances the belief arose that every mantra must have an "Om" in it. This belief was based on the overgeneralization of a particular sectarian concept. Even today the majority of the priests in India do not have formal training in the Sanskrit language. Many of them repeat any verse from anywhere, add a couple of "Oms" here and there, and claim that they are reciting mantras.

Customs and festivals are an integral part of culture. With the passage of time old customs are modified, new ones introduced, and our cultural activities and ceremonies change. But spirituality, unlike cultural activities and religious ceremonies, is constant. Just because some Sanskrit verses or folk songs contain a few mantric references does not mean that they are mantras. Reciting such verses has little or no spiritual significance.

On the other hand, a teacher trained by adepts neither consults a book nor depends on guesswork to impart a mantra. For her, the words of her master are the essence of the lineage. Such a teacher spontaneously feels which particular mantra is the best for a student. She does not depend on an aptitude test or intellectual analysis. The more energy she puts into analyzing a student's personality, problems, and concerns, and matching them with a mantra, the less connected she is with her master and with the lineage. In fact, choosing a mantra by means of intellectual analysis indicates that the initiator herself is a student rather than a teacher. Like a first-year medical student, she knows little about either the problem or the cure.

LAYING THE FOUNDATION

An intuitive, spontaneous flash is the best way for a teacher to know the most appropriate mantra to give, since at the time of initiation the teacher is fully aware of the presence of her master and feels that it is the master who is actually imparting the mantra. Because mantras coming from an unbroken lineage are already awakened, there is no need for elaborate rituals and auxiliary practices. As instructed by her master, the teacher simply explains how to meditate on that mantra, and what observances to follow. This is a guru mantra. We may not instantly gain a startling experience from it, but a process of self-transformation begins, and the higher virtues, such as love, compassion, and tolerance, inevitably unfold. Then, as these virtues blossom, they create the atmosphere for the next level of initiation. The teacher may then add something to the *bija* mantra or introduce an entirely new practice.

People sometimes wonder why experienced teachers teach

only a step at a time, instead of giving the entire instruction all at once. The reason is that if we undertake spiritual practice one step at a time we have less chance of slipping back. We encounter fewer obstacles, and those we do encounter can be more easily managed. The formula "Slow but steady wins the race" applies here. Moving at our own pace, we gain firsthand experience of inwardly observing how the seed sprouts, grows, blossoms, and bears fruit. We gain confidence as we notice how previous practices have laid the groundwork for those that follow.

Seed mantras are the locus for divine powers. Although their general function is divine protection, inner guidance, and cultivation of the power of determination, the powers unique to each mantra affect specific pranic currents and the unconscious contents of the deeper levels of the mind. Meditating on a seed mantra helps neutralize the effects of negative *samskaras* (subtle impressions of the past stored in the unconscious mind) and strengthens the positive ones. As discussed in chapter 3, some of these *samskaras* may be frightening or discouraging. So practicing just one or two seed mantras unveils only a limited number of these subtle impressions, and does so gradually rather than all at once.

The false images of ourselves that our egos create are the strongest of all mental contents. Meditating on the appropriate *bija* mantra gradually illuminates only those aspects of these false images that we can face positively and constructively. The gradual unfoldment of the inner self is always accompanied by the gradual disintegration of the false self, but the seed mantras give us the strength to stay composed when our self-imposed limitations begin to slide away. If this process occurs too quickly, attachment to the false self creates havoc. That is why intense *sadhana* is recommended only for those who are courageous, fearless, strong in body and mind, and—most importantly—firmly established in the principle of total surrender.

When the practice of the seed mantra has laid a firm foundation and our body, pranic vehicles, and mind are prepared, the teacher imparts the next level of initiation. This is the healthiest, safest, and surest way of advancing on the spiritual quest. Throughout this process we must remember that initiation and further instructions are the role of the teacher; our role is to practice. This means making a sincere effort to our fullest capacity. In this way the teacher's investment multiplies tenfold, thirtyfold, seventyfold, all the way to a hundredfold, as the Bible says.

We succeed in our practice when it is systematic and well balanced. It is advisable first to follow and master the basic principles of health and well-being outlined in Appendix A instead of jumping into a heavy practice. Once we have established a routine and have learned to regulate our life, then we can intensify our mantra practice.

SOME TIPS ON PRACTICE

Right after initiation it is a good idea to practice your mantra with mala beads, especially if the mantra is relatively long or consists of unfamiliar sounds. It takes a while for the mantra to create a strong groove in our mind, and until it does we have to make a conscious effort to repeat it and meditate on it.

A systematic approach to mantra meditation is to design a gradually increasing course of *japa* (a specific number of repetitions of mantra within a certain period of time). For example, the first week after initiation, commit yourself to doing one round of japa with your mala every day. Standard malas in the school of yoga consist of 108 beads. By doing one round of japa you will be repeating your mantra 108 times. If your mantra is short this may take five minutes or less. Then, if you have time and enjoy continuing your practice, listen to your mantra without using the beads.

The next week you can do two rounds, the third week three rounds, and so forth. Expand your practice until you reach either the limit of your capacity to sit comfortably or the limit of the time you have available. Maintain your practice at that level for three months. Then try meditating on your mantra for the same length of time without using your mala beads. Watch how your mind behaves. If you notice that you want to open your eyes, or look at your watch, you need to continue doing japa. Practicing japa prepares a solid ground for meditation. The more you practice japa, the more solid the ground.

Some techniques for holding the mala and turning the beads are more convenient than others. This one works very well: make a circle by lightly touching the tip of the thumb to the tip of the ring finger; hold the mala with the thumb and the third finger, gently supporting it with the ring finger. You may use any of these three fingers to turn the beads, although most students find turning them with the thumb easiest. The scriptures advise us not to use the index finger for doing japa.

If you are doing japa for a short period of time, hold the mala in front of the heart region. In a longer practice, however, this becomes tiresome and can create tension in your shoulders. When this happens, part of your mind automatically goes to the shoulders rather than focusing one-pointedly on the mantra. Furthermore, if your mala is made of heavy beads, the weight will be an added distraction. Therefore if you are doing a prolonged practice keep your hand on your knees or somewhere on your thighs, and do your japa comfortably there. It does not matter whether you hold the mala in the left hand or the right.

During initiation, good karmas are stirred up, creating a momentum for spiritual awakening. If you are comfortable doing japa for some time, the best way to take advantage of this momentum is to begin a methodical practice of japa called a *purash charana,* which involves completing a specific number of repetitions of a mantra in a designated period of time (45,000 repetitions of your mantra in forty-five days, for example). For a detailed description of *purash charana,* see Appendix B.

A self-imposed discipline such as a *purash charana* helps the student remain free of the deceptive tendencies of the mind. Without it the mind might say, "Well, I did enough today" or "Today I have lots of other work; I'll stop my practice here and catch up tomorrow." With *purash charana* you do not allow your mind to play such tricks. You have made a commitment to complete a specific number of repetitions of your mantra every day, and when you honor that commitment you attend to your *purash charana* and your *purash charana* attends to you. As a result, you and your mantra will become fast friends. How large a *purash charana* you should undertake depends on the length of your mantra, your capacity, and how much time you have at your disposal. An experienced teacher can guide you.

Whatever course of japa you undertake, it should be done with feeling. Dry repetition leads to boredom because the mind perceives it as monotonous; repeating your mantra while remaining aware of its meaning will create a feeling in your heart. However, being aware of the meaning of the mantra during meditation is a subtle process. First, assimilate the meaning of your mantra when you are not doing your formal japa or meditation practice. Ponder the meaning, relate it to yourself, and assimilate it in your heart and mind. When it matures, this contemplative exercise is transformed into pure awareness. Then you will not need to translate your mantra in order to get its meaning—mantra and meaning will flash simultaneously.

If you try to remember the literal meaning of your mantra you will disturb the process of meditation. The mantra is an unfamiliar sound and appears to be a word, so you may have a tendency to translate it into your own language. You may replace the mantra with one or more words in your native language, and then attempt to grasp its content from the translation. Avoid this tendency. Simply maintain the feeling of the mantra.

In a state of deep concentration only the feeling of the presence of the mantra remains—the individual syllables may be blurred. The logical mind, which perceives things in linear order, merges into pure, nonobjective awareness, comprehending spontaneously and in totality rather than in segments. That is why, in this state of awareness, the mantra remains but the mind is absorbed, and does not register every single syllable or phoneme.

It is wonderful if this happens, but make sure that this experience comes from deep meditation, not because you are spacing out. There is a subtle line between merging into nondualistic, nonobjective awareness and getting lost in oblivion. The sense of delight—the feeling that the burden of your mind is being lifted—is a sign of deep meditation. During such meditation your whole body is charged with the divine energy of your mantra, and afterwards you feel like a child of bliss—a princess or prince of freedom. If, on the other hand, you have been spacing out, your head will feel empty. You do not gain knowledge from a spacey state nor do you return a wiser person, as you do from deep meditation.

Until you have reached a deep state of meditation, therefore, make a conscious effort to remember every single syllable of your mantra distinctly. Gradually, articulation of the mantra becomes secondary and *bhava* (pure feeling) takes over. This is how mantra becomes refined until its articulate form merges into pure feeling—the *vaikhari* (articulate form of mantra) merges into *madhyama* (mantra in the form of the thought-force). Then, as the mantra becomes more refined and subtle, the next step manifests: *madhyama* merges into *pashyanti* (the purest and most silent form of mantra). The *pashyanti* state of mantra is known as *anahata nada*, "the unstruck sound." The mantras were revealed to the seers at this level; they will lead our consciousness there.

Just as the entire universe issues

forth from the Primordial Being, so

do numberless mantras in their

manifest and unmanifest form. . . .

If secrecy is maintained, mantras

bear their fruit, but once exposed,

the fruit is lost.

Netra Tantra 14:6, 9, 11

C H A P T E R   6

Classes of Mantras and Their Powers

F lowing forth from the highest source, mantra *shakti* descends into the consciousness of the sages and assumes a body made of sound. This is the genesis of numberless mantras. Based on the phonemes of which they are composed, they emerge in various forms, some long, some short; depending on the intrinsic characteristics of their constituent sounds, they carry different powers and have different transformative functions. In general, however, they fall into six categories: meditative mantras, contemplative mantras, *siddha* mantras, *maha* mantras, *apta* mantras, and *sabar* mantras.

Meditative Mantras

Meditative mantras are focal points of pure spiritual energy. When we meditate on them, they bring about spiritual illumination. Thus, they are bridges by which we can cross the mire of delusion and reach the other shore. All spiritual traditions rooted in the Vedas permit teachers to impart the mantras of this category as guru mantras. Teachers belonging to non-Vedic traditions and teachers interested in miracles, healing, and *siddhis* may, on the other hand, impart non-meditative mantras as guru mantras.

In the West, the mantras students receive during initiation are often mistakenly called personal mantras. They are personal only in the sense that a student receives them in a private initiation directly from a teacher; in truth they are guru mantras. This term is of great significance. *Gu* means "the darkness of ignorance," and *ru* means "that which dispels." Thus, *guru* is the force that dispels the darkness of ignorance. The literal meaning of *mantra* is "that which guides our thought-force with full protection." Thus, dispelling the darkness of ignorance and protecting the mind while leading it into the deeper dimensions of life are the basic functions of a guru mantra. It is both a sword and a shield: it cuts potential obstacles asunder, and it wards off all dangers.

Because they are imbued with the power of inner guidance and divine protection, meditative, or guru, mantras help us transform our unconscious mind. A master knows how powerful habit patterns are, the hold they have on our conscious mind and senses, and how deeply human beings are affected by the fear of death. So at the time of initiation he imparts a mantra that can attenuate and eventually erase our negative habit patterns and enable us to overcome our fear. A guru mantra is an eternal friend, guiding us both here and hereafter.

The purpose of practicing a meditative mantra is to attain enlightenment. Unlike other sacred sounds, its power does not become diffused. Rather, as we continue practicing, the energy generated by this mantra gradually condenses, purifying our mind and heart. And as the practice intensifies, this subtle energy disperses, energizing our surroundings. External as well as internal realms are transformed by the intense practice of a guru mantra. My master, Sri Swami Rama of the Himalayas, recounts the following story that illustrates the power of meditative mantras:

In the city of Kanpur in India there lived a saintly woman. Sensing that she did not have much longer to live, she secluded herself in her room and focused on remembering the guru mantra in which she was initiated. Six months later she fell ill, and the time of her parting seemed imminent. All the members of her family loved her and, not knowing what else to do, they wanted to be near her and to attend to her all the time. But she wanted to be alone with her mantra.

So one day she told her son, "Please don't be attached to me. On this path, everyone walks alone. The name of the Lord is with me. I am in great joy; nothing can bind me to this mortal plane."

Her son cried, "Don't you still love me? You are my mother."

She replied, "That which was supposed to happen has already happened. I am free from all fears and anxieties. You are attached to this mortal body, but this is just a shell—and you call it 'Mother.'"

Her family respected her last wish, and she left her body peacefully. After her death, Swamiji writes, "The walls of that room in which she lived vibrated with the sound of her mantra. Anyone who came in could feel the sound emanating from those walls. Someone informed me that the walls of that house were still radiating her mantra. I could not believe it. So I visited the house, and it was true. The sound of her mantra was still vibrating there."

By constantly repeating and meditating on her mantra, a meditator fortifies her inner world, and the mantra creates a new reality. After death a meditator goes neither to hell nor to heaven; rather, after the body falls apart she merges with her mantra. Her awareness is not trapped in the unconscious mind, as usually happens, but dissolves into mantra *shakti*. And under the guidance of the Divine such a blessed meditator will emerge again from that same mantra only to complete her remaining journey, to help others, or both.

CONTEMPLATIVE MANTRAS

Most contemplative mantras come from the Upanishads. They are known as *maha vakyas* (great sentences or utterances)—brief, terse, and profound phrases imbued with unimaginable philosophical insight. They are used for self-analysis, self-reflection, and—ultimately—Self-realization.

According to the Vedantic tradition, the most important prerequisite to the practice of contemplative mantras is the profound study of philosophy under the guidance of a competent teacher. However, intellectual study of philosophical texts is a reliable means for Self-realization only if a seeker has already cultivated a sixfold spiritual wealth: tranquility, self-restraint, forbearance, transcendence of sensual pleasure, lack of inner conflict, and the desire for liberation.

Contemplative mantras are usually a central part of the

practice given to aspirants on the path of renunciation. Rather than focusing on the sound of the mantra, the aspirant allows her mind to flow along the current of the philosophical thought it contains. Thus it is necessary to understand the exact meaning of the mantra so clearly and deeply that it flashes in the mind with perfection and precision.

This is the path of Vedanta, said to be "the razor's edge," the most difficult of all paths. People with inadequate intellectual training have a hard time penetrating the meaning of the mantras, whereas intellectuals risk falling into pedantry. Following this path requires relating the sublime truth imbedded in the mantra to ourselves. For example, *so'ham* is a *maha vakya* meaning "I am That." When we use it as a tool for concentrating the mind, we synchronize the sound with our breath, as described in chapter 4. But when *so'ham* is used as a contemplative mantra, we focus on the meaning, "I am That," examining how this meaning can transform our worldview and bring about a qualitative change in the circumstances of our life.

On this path, non-possessiveness and non-attachment must bloom before we can attain the highest illumination, but the subtleties of these two traits cannot be quantified in terms of material accumulation and external behavior. These virtues unfold as we contemplate and truly understand the transitory nature of worldly objects and realize not only that it is a waste of time to pursue them, but also that entangling ourselves with these tantalizing objects is painful. With this realization, the mind loses interest in running into the external world and turns inward. Then, from time to time, it catches glimpses of the inner Self. The more sustained these glimpses, the less delight the mind finds in worldly objects and sense pleasures. Non-possessiveness and non-attachment begin to unfold naturally. And the more these virtues grow, the more time and energy we find to explore the deeper dimensions of life.

We can discern whether we are actually experiencing a sense of non-possessiveness and non-attachment, or just pretending to, only through self-study and self-observation. I came to understand this when I was completing work on my doctoral dissertation.

In the course of doing research I had to visit the Sanskrit University library in Benares. My professor knew of my interest in swamis and yogis, so he told me that I must meet a swami who lived in one of the monasteries near Durga Kunda in Benares. I visited him one afternoon and was so impressed with his teaching that I began to attend his discourses regularly.

As I spent more time at the swami's ashram, I was even more impressed to see that he owned nothing—only a couple of burlap loincloths and a water vessel. His bed was made of several layers of burlap, and his pillow was a bundle of the same material. People respected him because he never touched money with his own hands, and women could see him only from a distance. But as I drew closer to him, I began to notice a conflict between his actions and his words. He was teaching non-possessiveness and non-attachment, but was he practicing it?

I thought at first it was my own negative mind that was forcing me to imagine shortcomings in others, and each time I saw something that raised doubts, I condemned myself. A couple of times I even confessed my doubts to the swami. I repeatedly told myself that I had come to study with this great man, not to weigh his merits or demerits.

One evening, as usual, he sent one of his students to get a two-rupee bill and buy milk for the evening tea, giving precise instructions as to where to find the bill. "It is between the third and the fourth layer of the burlap bed on the left side of the pillow," he said.

The student searched for the bill in vain. "Maharaj-ji, I couldn't find a two-rupee bill between the third and fourth layer on the left side of the pillow, but there were many other two-rupee bills in other parts of the bed."

The swami seemed annoyed. "How is it possible?" he asked. "Where can it go?"

So the swami and the student went to the bedroom together. Out of curiosity, skepticism, and mischief, I followed them. The swami ordered the student to turn back first one layer of burlap and then another on the left-hand corner, and then both layers on the right-hand corner. The student found several two-rupee bills, but the swami kept saying, "No, no. The one I'm talking about was not as wrinkled as this one. It was newer, and one of its corners was slightly folded."

As I watched, the swami became enraged. The students were frightened, but I was determined to know the truth: Was the swami affected by the apparent loss of the money, or was he teaching a lesson? Part of me thought he might be trying to demonstrate his intuitive ability to know things without touching and looking at them, or maybe he was demonstrating his extraordinary retentive power. But another part of myself whispered, Don't you see—he is really perturbed? I thought, Let this be my last day of living with inner conflict and doubt. So I pulled a two-rupee bill from my pocket so that everyone could see it clearly. Handing it to the student, I said, "Brahmachariji, forget all this. Take these rupees and buy the milk." The swami calmed down instantly and the atmosphere returned to normal. A couple of minutes later I touched the swami's feet and asked permission to leave.

The swami said, "No, no, Sonny. Stay awhile. Have your tea, and then go."

I humbly replied, "It will be too late, Swamiji." I left the ashram and never went back.

As Swami Rama writes, "Even after renouncing wealth, home, relatives, wife, and children, one cannot easily renounce the lust for name and fame, nor can one easily purify the ego and direct the emotions toward Self-realization. Cultivating a new mind is the necessary step for enlightenment. Mere renunciation brings unhappiness and frustration."

No matter how clearly and directly the master has imparted contemplative mantras, and no matter how much time we spend contemplating their meanings, we experience spiritual advancement only when we commit ourselves to self-discipline. Without discipline, this process is mere brooding, not contemplation. But with self-discipline as a vehicle, these mantras lead us through gradually advancing stages of self-training that help us gain and retain the direct experience of the truth contained in the contemplative mantras. This in turn expands our awareness and helps us accomplish the purpose of life.

SIDDHA MANTRAS

There are certain mantras capable of either awakening supernatural powers within or evoking nature's forces without—although they may or may not have a spiritual value. Mantras of this category are usually for developing *siddhis,* such as reading others' minds, knowing past and future, and awakening healing power. These are awakened mantras. The adepts of the mantra tradition have kept their energy active. The thousands of mantras mentioned in the Tantric scriptures are *siddha* mantras, but most of them are dormant, and doing japa or meditating on dormant mantras is like trying to cook a meal using a small pile of matchsticks. Scholars and seekers who are not connected with the spiritual tradition often employ elaborate rituals, recitations of scripture, fasting, and devotional acts in an attempt to awaken the energy of these *siddha* mantras. Sometimes it works, but in most cases it does not.

It is said that those who have *siddha* mantras do not teach them; only those who do not have them teach them. Students who have not been initiated by an authorized teacher may pick up a *siddha* mantra from a book, practice it and gain little or nothing, and no harm is done. But if a student who has been initiated and thus is connected with the lineage does this, the consequences can be serious because the *siddha* mantras recognize the student's connection and may unfold their powers before the practitioner is fully prepared to assimilate them.

Swami Rama shares one such experience in *Living with the Himalayan Masters.* At the time these events took place, Swamiji was traveling with his master, who had a manuscript to which access was strictly prohibited—he had made a point of telling Swamiji that he should not experiment with this manuscript. Realizing it was very special, Swamiji, who was young and mischievous, felt that he must read it; after all, if he got in trouble he knew his master would help him.

So one evening, while his master was resting in a hut on the bank of the Ganges, Swamiji saw his chance. The hut had no windows and only one door, so he locked his master in, unwrapped the manuscript, and began to read it by the light of the full moon. He was awestruck when he came upon a certain practice, along with the description of the experience it would induce, and decided to experiment with it, even though according to the scripture the practice was to be undertaken only by advanced yogis and could be dangerous if not done properly.

The practice involved repeating a special mantra 1,001 times in a particular style while performing certain rituals. Swamiji began to repeat the mantra, completing 900 repetitions without noticing any effect. But when he arrived at the 940th repetition, he noticed a huge woman making a fire nearby. By the time she had brought a large vessel of water on the fire to a boil, Swamiji had completed 970 repetitions. Then he lost count as an enormous man approached. Thinking this was the effect of the mantra he was repeating, Swamiji told himself to focus on the japa and ignore what seemed to be happening near him. But anxiety led him to open his eyes, and he was frightened to see that the gigantic man was completely naked and walking toward him. The man asked the woman, "What have you cooked for me?"

She said, "I have nothing. If you give me something I'll cook it."

The giant man pointed at Swamiji and said, "Look at him sitting over there. Why don't you cut him into pieces and cook him?"

Hearing that, Swamiji's teeth clenched, the mala dropped from his hand, and he fainted. He eventually regained consciousness, to find his master slapping him and telling him to wake up. Swamiji became conscious for a moment, and then the memory of that dreadful scene came forward, and he fainted again. This happened three or four times. Finally his master kicked him and said, "Get up! Why did you do this? I told you not to practice these mantras. And you locked me in, you foolish boy."

From Swamiji's experience we get some inkling of the power of *siddha* mantras. Only after our mind is settled in the guru mantra is it safe to undertake the practice of *siddha* mantras. When practiced without due preparation, they can cause hallucinations, and hallucinating is not a spiritual experience—it is a sign that an energy has been evoked in a disorganized manner by an impure and untrained mind. Only a purified and inwardly directed mind can withstand the flood of energy that rushes forth from the *siddha* mantras. Here a master's permission and guidance are of the utmost importance.

MAHA MANTRAS

Maha mantras, also called *maha vidyas,* are the most potent and highly secret distillation of all mantras. Every *maha vidya* has a complete system of *sadhana* to accompany it, and a unique metaphysical foundation. *Maha* mantras are not openly written in the scriptures, nor do experienced commentators or authors of independent treatises render them clearly. They are never pronounced in the casual course of study, but are referred to by their specific names.

The practice of the *maha vidyas* can be done only by those who have trained their body with a systematic practice of hatha yoga, who have transformed their force of emotion into love and devotion, and who have sharpened their intellect to comprehend the terse and abstruse philosophical doctrines that stand behind these powerful mantras. The aspirant who successfully ventures on this path must have a perfect blend of faith and reason, love and knowledge, compassion and discrimination, tenderness in feelings and strictness in discipline, and—most importantly—limitless self-effort and God's grace.

It is utterly impossible to gain a complete understanding of this science only by doing a technically correct repetition of the mantra, or only by studying the scriptures—both are required. Similarly, the contemplative part of the practice must be balanced with yogic disciplines that bring the forces of body, breath, and mind into a state of perfect balance.

Since the practice of the *maha vidyas* evokes forces outside and inside the body and mind simultaneously, the aspirant must proceed one step at a time in order to assimilate the experience. The first step is to study the scriptures and gain a clear intellectual understanding of the science and its philosophical foundation. What is more, if we aspire to tread this path we cannot expect the masters of the *maha vidyas* to teach us the scriptures—we must complete a major part of the study on our own. And because access to the scriptures requires a solid knowledge of Sanskrit, lack of proficiency in this language is the greatest obstacle.

The second step on this path is initiation into a guru mantra. Meditating on it fortifies the body and mind, and only when we have accomplished this does a learned master give us the third step—initiation into one of the *maha* mantras.

While assimilating the third step, we expand our knowledge of the practice. As the theory becomes clear, the master grants permission to practice the external rituals that go along with the *maha* mantras. This is the fourth step. To the majority of students, ritual worship is extremely helpful. It is like a stepping stone enabling us to transcend body consciousness and penetrate the inner realm. It purifies and harmonizes the surrounding environment and helps create the psychological conditions appropriate for invoking and greeting the divine force within and without.

As these psychological conditions manifest, we come to realize the importance of meditating on auxiliary mantras and the forces of nature to which they correspond. We come to realize that there are numberless currents and crosscurrents in the stream of life, and that Self-realization in its truest sense means knowing the stream of life in its totality and perfection. That is why the adepts of *maha vidyas* are also well versed in the dynamics of the *anga vidyas* (the mantras that are complementary to the main *maha* mantras).

According to *mantra vedins* (the knowers of mantra science), the relationship between *maha vidya* and *anga vidya* is that of the whole body to its parts. Keeping the body healthy and functional requires paying attention to every limb and organ, because all must function in perfect coordination. Similarly, the aspirant must know how the different *anga vidyas* relate to the *maha* mantra and how they function. Tantra and Agama scriptures explain how numberless waves of the life-force emerge from and subside into the one, nondual, divine force. The *maha* mantra is identical to this force, and the secondary mantras are the numerous currents and crosscurrents which constitute life. If this realization does not dawn, the practice becomes technical and dry.

During my research I met only a few devout practitioners of the *maha vidyas*. Discussions with them revealed that they were not clear about the exact method of practice they had undertaken. Because they had not gotten clear and definitive instructions from their teachers, they had relied on books which were obscure and often contradictory. Furthermore, most of these practitioners used the *maha* mantras and their complementary mantras only as a means for worshiping a deity. The purpose of deity worship, however, is to cultivate love and devotion. This channels the power of emotion inward rather than outward. If mantras are used as a means for external worship, a practitioner will become a worshiper, but not necessarily a yogi. I met several worshipers of *maha vidyas,* but rarely did I encounter an adept of *maha vidya* who also followed the path of yoga.

According to yoga, the goal of practicing the *maha* mantras is to attain a state of oneness with them. As the experience of oneness between the seeker's consciousness and the *maha* mantra reaches fruition, the sense of separateness between guru, disciple, mantra, and the highest reality disappears. But long before the aspirant attains this experience of unitary consciousness, supernatural powers begin to unfold. If the aspirant has not attained mastery over her body, breath, and mind with the help of hatha yoga *mudras,* of *pranayamas,* and— most importantly—of *vairagya* (dispassion), then she may not be able to assimilate the extraordinary experiences which manifest during these practices. Such a one may end up with imbalanced energies in body and mind. As a result, even if she is blessed with profound knowledge and a compelling aura, she may not remain healthy or normal. That is why the scriptures clearly say that no matter how advanced you are, you must practice under the guidance of a master. The following story illustrates this point.

There is a *shakti* shrine in the Mirzapur district of northern India known as Vindhya Vasani. It lies on the northern tip of the Vindhya Range. Not too long ago a famous swami called Akshobhyananda lived there. He was said to be a devout practitioner of the *maha vidya* known as Tara. While following the path of *kaula* tantra (the path that employs ritualistic techniques), he meditated with full sincerity on this *maha* mantra and, as the practice became intense, the power of the mantra materialized and a personified form of Tara emerged. But the swami was unable to assimilate this extraordinary vision; he became disoriented and remained that way. Without warning, for example, he would see the personified form of the goddess and run toward her, uncontrolled and unconscious, colliding with trees and boulders. Internally, he may have been in a state of bliss, but externally he was schizophrenic, to use the language of modern psychology.

The practice of the *maha* mantras is the highest practice in mantra *sadhana*. But it is very systematic and precise, and requires constant guidance from a competent master. Techniques described in the scriptures of kundalini and Tantra yoga form the disciplinary basis for practicing these powerful mantras.

APTA MANTRAS

Apta mantras are uniquely associated with the sage who imparts them. They may look and sound like ordinary words or phrases, but they are mantras because they have been uttered by a sage of pure heart and extraordinary divine power. They manifest their potentials in the precise manner determined by the sage, and there are no rules about how to receive and practice them. One of the experiences Swami Rama shares in *Living with the Himalayan Masters* will help us gain some insight into what *apta* mantras are and how they work.

At the direction of his master, Swamiji went to study with a saint who lived across the river in Rishikesh. As a part of the routine of that saint's ashram, everyone would get up early in the morning, complete their ablutions, and wash their hands and feet in the Ganges. Then one of the disciples would climb a tree and pull off a branch in order to make toothbrushes. This is the standard system of brushing your teeth in India. You chew one end of a twig until the fibers are crushed; then you brush your teeth; when you finish, you split the twig and scrape your tongue with the sharp edge.

One day the saint, who was quite old, climbed the tree himself. There was a beehive in the tree, but he continued climbing until he reached it. Then he started talking to the bees. Looking up at him, Swamiji shouted, "Please, Swamiji, don't disturb them! They are wild bees. They will sting you and then sting all of us."

The saint ignored him and pulled off a branch right by the hive. The bees did not bother him. When he came down he told Swamiji to climb up and pluck a branch for himself.

Swamiji replied, "No, no, Sir. I can live without one." Then, thinking that the saint must have had a special mantra to calm the bees, he added, "But if you really want me to climb this tree, please tell me the mantra that protected you."

The saint told Swamiji that if Swamiji climbed the tree, he would tell him the mantra. So Swamiji climbed. From the ground, the saint instructed him, "Go nearer and talk to them face to face. Tell them, 'I live here alongside you and I don't harm you. Don't harm me.'"

Swamiji argued, "That's not a mantra."

The saint replied, "Better you do as I say. Talk to the bees. Your lips should be close enough so that they can hear you whisper."

Although Swamiji was skeptical, he did exactly as the saint

instructed him and the bees did not attack. When he came down, the saint laughed and said, "Do not impart this mantra to anyone, for it will work only for you. And don't forget what I am telling you."

In the weeks that followed Swamiji took honey from many hives, but the bees never stung him; people were impressed with this ability. Then one day in the state of Punjab a goldsmith who knew him well requested the bee mantra. Somehow Swamiji had forgotten what the saint had told him—that it would not work for anyone else. So he told the goldsmith how to talk to bees, and under Swamiji's guidance the man climbed up to a hive and repeated the mantra. Hundreds of bees attacked him. He fell from the tree and was taken to the hospital, where he remained in a coma for three days. All Swamiji could do was pray for him.

On the third day after this incident, the saint appeared at the hospital, scolded Swamiji, and finally said, "Let this be a final lesson to you. The man will recover in the morning. But I am withdrawing the power of this mantra from you. You can never use it again."

Swamiji concludes the story with these words: "Sometimes the words of a great man can have the effect of a mantra. Whenever any great man speaks to you, you should accept his words as mantras and practice them." Thus, the words from the mouth of a saint are called *apta* mantras.

SABAR MANTRAS

Mantras whose source is unidentifiable are classified as *sabar* mantras. They can be found in any language. In fact, they sometimes contain words, phrases, concepts and expressions from a vast range of languages and geographic regions. For example, a *sabar* mantra can contain an Arabic word, an Islamic concept, and a word, a phrase, or even a seed mantra from the Vedic or Tantric tradition, while its overall structure is in Bengali.

There are a number of opinions about *sabar* mantras. For example, sacred sounds revealed to holy men of tribal communities are called *sabar* mantras. Mantras which are not found in a philosophical doctrine or in prominent scriptures belonging to one of the recognized traditions, such as Vedic, Upanishadic, Jaina, or Buddhist, are also *sabar* mantras. Spiritual seekers consider mantras that are not in Sanskrit to be *sabar* mantras. According to such seekers, Lord Shiva manifested these mantras for the welfare of human beings at the request of Parvati, his consort. Laypeople throughout India, Nepal, Tibet, China, Cambodia, Burma, Indonesia, Thailand, and Sri Lanka use *sabar* mantras for a variety of purposes, such as overcoming fever, curing phobias, removing sleep- and food-related disorders, or healing someone who has been bitten by a snake. In these regions *sabar* mantras transcend the boundaries of religion and creed—Hindus, Muslims, Buddhists, Sikhs, Sufis, Christians, and Parsees believe in the miraculous powers of these sacred sounds.

Sabar mantras usually consist of monotonous, often redundant sounds interspersed with words belonging to one of the modern languages or their older counterparts. Each mantra has its own unique obligatory observances. For example, one mantra can be repeated only in the night, another only while you are facing east, still another only during a lunar eclipse. In most cases, the standard prerequisites of meditation do not apply—an erect posture, serene breath, and one-pointed mind are not as important here as following the exact instructions given by the person who imparted the *sabar* mantra, regardless of whether or not these instructions seem to make any sense. *Sabar* mantras are for mundane purposes, not for knowledge, liberation, or enlightenment.

SEALING THE HOLES IN THE MIND

In the realm of spiritual practice, learned teachers generally recommend only meditative, contemplative, and *siddha* mantras. The *maha* mantras are imparted only after long and thorough preparation. *Apta* and *sabar* mantras in most cases are meant for mundane purposes and not for spiritual upliftment.

In the yoga tradition teachers will often impart a seed mantra, but seem to be less generous beyond that point. This is because at the higher levels of initiation, meditation begins to wear an esoteric garb, and the spiritual journey may not be very convincing intellectually. We understand the value of the higher levels of mantra *sadhana* only when we rise above the domain of intellect and begin seeing through the eye of the heart. The journey to this domain requires complete openness, willingness, and receptivity. It demands that we make a sincere effort to our utmost capacity, without harboring the slightest doubt.

Doubt is the worst enemy of a seeker. It is like an army of

termites eating away the foundation, causing the entire structure to collapse. For this reason it is impossible to receive a higher initiation in mantra *sadhana* if any doubt lingers in the mind. The ever-guiding divine force that flows through an unbroken guru-disciple lineage does not allow a teacher to impart an invaluable mantra to someone whose mind and heart are full of holes. From the womb of doubt, insecurity, fear, and anxiety arise, and this trio eats away at our motivation and sows the seeds of sloth, inertia, and irregular practice—making it impossible for us to contain divine wealth.

Many of us long for a higher initiation while we still harbor some degree of doubt about either the teacher, his teachings, or both. Consequently we neither study with an open mind nor practice wholeheartedly. Then we wonder why we are not miraculously transformed. This is a common obstacle. Introspection and the company of wise people are the most effective ways to overcome it. Introspection consists of self-analysis, self-observation, and—most importantly—a genuine desire to commit ourselves to self-discipline as well as the courage to do so. We can take full advantage of the company of wise people only when we have cultivated patience, forbearance, and a strong desire to attain the highest good.

This is why the scriptures and the masters constantly tell us, "Seal the holes in your mind." The sages of the Upanishads say that all holes can be sealed by cultivating the following six virtues: *shama* (quietude of mind), *dama* (self-restraint), *titiksha* (forbearance), *uparati* (indifference toward sensual pleasures), *samadhana* (transcending conflicts), and *mumuksha* (the desire for liberation). As these virtues unfold, we begin to mature as students.

My own experience has taught me that a master skillfully ignores the demands and requests that we make prematurely. On the other hand, when the time is right, he is very generous in teaching higher practices, and does not wait for us to make a verbal request.

Those whose minds are scattered

and dense have no way of finding

the subtle path of kundalini. To

deliver them, O Divine Mother,

you assume numerous external

and tangible forms which can

be perceived by the senses and

ordinary mind.

Tripura Rahasya,
Mahatmya Khanda 30:24

C H A P T E R 7

M A N T R A ,   Y A N T R A ,   A N D   D E I T Y

Many spiritual traditions, among them the Vedic, biblical, and Talmudic, tell us that two inseparable streams of divine sound and light *(nada* and *bindu)* spring forth from Pure Consciousness. In this way the inner truth travels outward, manifesting as the world of multiple names and forms. The journey inward can also be accomplished by using either of these vehicles: there is a perfect equation between the divine sound embodied in mantra and the divine light embodied in forms such as yantras, mandalas, and deities.

Where we begin our spiritual quest is determined by our culture and our circumstances. Some of us start with the Vedas and the Upanishads, others with the Bible or the Koran, others with the Torah or Buddhist texts, and still others with tapes and books on New Age spirituality or holistic health. Regardless of where we begin, we eventually reach the point at which all paths converge into one path with two parallel tracks: nada and bindu.

All paths that incorporate sacred sound are grounded in nada—the tradition of primordial sound. And all paths that employ sacred forms—such as yantras (geometrical diagrams) or personified forms (deities)—and center their spiritual disciplines around symbols and images are offshoots of bindu. According to the yoga tradition, the human body is actually the crystallization of sound and light; it is the locus of all mantras, yantras, mandalas, and deities. Every cell is the result of an orchestration of sound and light, and the adepts of the *maha vidyas* (more specifically the adepts of Sri Vidya) know which of these energy waves lead to Pure Consciousness.

SHIVA AND SHAKTI

A systematic study of nada and bindu helps us to understand not only the perfect equation between mantra and yantra, but also the relationships between the higher forces in the human body and the cosmic forces that we call gods, goddesses, and deities. Such a study can also help us understand the role of mantra shakti in awakening kundalini. However, the most profound study of the relationships among mantra, yantra, deity, and kundalini shakti is found in the spiritual tradition of Sri Vidya. In the Sri Vidya tradition all these concepts are indicated by such terms as *sri mata, chitkala, samaya,* or *spanda shakti.*

Spanda shakti refers to the eternal power intrinsic to Pure Consciousness. According to mantra *shastra,* consciousness is Shiva and the vibrant energy intrinsic to it is Shakti; they are two inseparable aspects of the same reality: consciousness and the power of consciousness. Consciousness is unmanifest potential energy; it manifests as kinetic energy. That is why the scriptures say that Shiva and Shakti are one and the same—Shiva dwells in Shakti, and vice versa.

As used in this context, Shiva and Shakti are not to be confused with the Hindu god and goddess who, according to mythology, live on Mt. Kailasa. Here we are concerned with the metaphysics of mantra science, not with mythology or theology. According to this science, the process of the manifestation, maintenance, and dissolution of the universe is carried out by Shakti, the divine, creative power of Shiva. Shiva is the static force behind Shakti's creative power. The relationship between the two is that of sunlight and sun, of heat and fire. One cannot exist without the other.

Although Shiva is described as motionless, static consciousness, this consciousness is actually in perpetual motion because of the vibrant, creative force intrinsic to it: *spanda shakti* (loosely translated as "vibration"). In some scriptures, *spanda shakti* is also known as *anahata nada* (the unstruck sound). This state of vibration and the energy emitted by it are beyond the comprehension of the senses and mind. Only those yogis who have crossed the boundaries of time, space, and causation and have attained a state of mindless mind can hear the pure vibration of the unstruck sound. This is a matter of inner experience, but for the sake of our understanding, the yogis have attempted to convey a sense of this inner sound by comparing it to audible sounds. For example, they tell us that the first stage of inner sound is similar to the sound of a pin or a small nail dropping. At the second stage, the pitch is slightly deeper. At the third and final state—the stage of nada—the sound is similar to that produced by the horn used in Jewish rituals. Parallel to *anahata nada*, and emerging simultaneously, the yogis also discovered the inner light manifesting in different degrees and grades.

According to mantra science, when the inner sound and light become outwardly oriented, they assume gradually grosser forms. What we perceive as solid matter is merely this energy vibrating at a rate that appears solid to our senses. Different vibrational frequencies lend diversity to the manifest world, but the vibrationless vibration of *spanda* is the primordial and most basic energy. All other forms of energy pervading and composing the universe are simply manifestations of this vibrationless vibration of Pure Consciousness.

This universe and everything in it are like a wave arising from the blissful ocean of *spanda shakti* and subsiding into it again. In other words, the entire universe is an ocean of blissful vibration, ranging from the ultra-deep notes generated by the spiraling of the Milky Way, to the medium-range notes produced by a piano, to the inaudible frequencies produced by our brain waves, to the ultra-fast frequencies of light and other forms of cosmic energy. The principles of resonance and harmony are the basis of this vibratory universe. Just as in music an understanding of the structure and meaning of one octave provides insight into all other octaves, a complete understanding of either the universe as a whole or an individual entity can be gained by experiencing the increasingly subtle vibratory patterns of *spanda shakti* manifesting as energy, matter, mind, and the individual self.

Just as the spectrum of visible light gives the impression of whiteness when it is viewed as a whole, so the undifferentiated spectrum of sound is experienced as white sound. The principal channel of this spectrum of vibration in the human body is *sushumna*, the central energy channel situated in the innermost space in the spinal cord. Here, energy is absorbed and emitted as *sushumna* broadcasts its unique frequency to the rest of the body. The scriptures describe this energy as a white dot, *sita bindu;* it is consciously experienced only by yogis.

The energy channel running on the left of *sushumna* is *ida* and the channel on the right is *pingala*. The energies traveling through these channels are characterized as lunar and solar, passive and active, female and male, respectively. They are also described as being blue and red; thus the energy of ida is called *asita bindu* (the blue dot) and the energy of pingala is *rakta bindu* (the red dot). The energies traveling through all the other channels in the human body interact either negatively or positively and in varying intensities with either the blue dot or the red dot, creating a numberless combination of currents and crosscurrents of energy. This, in turn, causes vibratory patterns to manifest in varying frequencies. Finally, matter emerges in different forms, shapes, and colors along the patterns of these subtle energies.

We take for granted the translation of sound from one form to another in the phenomenal world. For example, when Beethoven intuited the currents of inner sound—nada—he was able to express them on paper. His compositions are the musical form of his experience. Musicians take a copy of

Beethoven's score and produce mechanical vibrations in musical instruments, which in turn set up resonant vibrations in the molecules of the air, which are then transmitted into a microphone. The electrical impulses in the microphone modulate the electromagnetic waves, which are broadcast from a radio transmitter. These vibrations in turn pass through the atmosphere and set up resonant frequencies in a radio receiver miles away, where they are rectified and amplified, creating a resonant vibration that is transmitted to the eardrum and through bone and fluid into the sensitive inner ear. Vibrations in the inner ear are transformed into neural impulses, which are transmitted along the auditory nerve into the brain. These electrochemical vibrations are then carried through biokinetic stages to the perceptual level of our personality. Thus, the mind resonates with the original form experienced by Beethoven.

We rarely stop to think that there are dozens of invisible steps involved when we hear and enjoy Beethoven's music. Similarly, the unstruck sound goes through various modifications before it is perceived by the sages and transmitted to us as mantras, although how this occurs is a mystery that cannot be solved by the mind and the senses. These mantras are infinitely more subtle than our nervous system, senses, brain, and ordinary mind can perceive. When these profound mantric experiences first unfolded, however, the sages, in deep *samadhi,* received a simultaneous revelation that enabled them to comprehend an articulate and audible sound in perfect resonance with the soundless sound of the mantra. In some cases they also received a visual form of the mantra, thus yielding yantras, chakras, and mandalas.

Because sound and form are inseparable, mantras are often inscribed on yantras. We have seen that the Word can be traced back to the primeval divine force from which both words and the objects denoted by them emerge. Form in its essence is sound, and sound in its gross state is form. Thus, speaking metaphysically, yantras and mantras are one and the same—yantra is the gross form of mantra, and mantra is a subtle form of yantra. Both operate on subtle principles of physics that are similar to those governing the conversion of energy into matter, and matter into energy.

YANTRAS

Like meditative mantras, of which they are the visual form, yantras have the power to lead us through the steps of spiritual evolution to the experience of Ultimate Reality. Yantras are geometrical diagrams, intuitively perceived during the inner journey of sages, and if understood properly, they can unveil the mystical experience of the original seers. Just as modern scientists have developed mathematical equations and laws to describe the workings of the universe, so did the sages—the ancient scientists of the inner realm—use their immense powers of introspection to discover forms that express the underlying order, structure, and dynamics of both the phenomenal and the spiritual worlds. Just as physicists use equations and theorems, so have the sages used yantras. Like the numbers and symbols in an equation, circles and lines in a yantra contain profound meaning. To someone ignorant of physics, the equations $E=mc^2$ or $F=ma$ are letters and numbers with little meaning. But to physicists, these are powerful formulas that profoundly enhance their understanding of the nature and dynamics of the universe. In the same way, a yantra is a visual equation of the energies governing both the internal and the external worlds; the practitioner who fully understands the language of yantras has this energy at his command and comprehends the subtle dynamics of both these worlds.

The word *yantra* is derived from the Sanskrit verb root *yam,* which means "to sustain, hold, support, govern, or control." Thus, a yantra is a concentrated field of consciousness that pulls together and controls different types of energies. According to yogis, certain yantras, especially those corresponding to the mantras of the *maha vidyas,* uphold, sustain, guide, and govern the entire range of primordial energy—*spanda shakti.* Yantras are not merely symbols of the primal archetypal forms of manifestation, they are the actual manifest forms of *spanda shakti* and have the power to govern the energies they contain.

Yantras are generally composed of a bindu, triangles, circles, squares, lotuses, and seed mantras—each of which is symbolic. The bindu is its most important component. Represented by a dot at the center of the yantra, this is the nucleus from which the kinetic energy radiates, reaching the outer circumference before subsiding again into the nucleus. The bindu is also the symbolic representation of the all-embracing reservoir of infinite energy and consciousness. It is the seed of the universe. In metaphysical terms it is the unitary state of Shakti and Shiva. From a spiritual point of view it is the *sahasrara*, the thousand-petaled lotus at the crown chakra that is the center of Supreme Consciousness.

In a yantra, the triangle is the symbol for the cosmic place where the rhythmic flow of creative energy crystallizes. Because space cannot be bound by fewer than three lines, the triangle also symbolizes the creative burst, the root matrix of nature (*mula-trikona*). A triangle with its apex pointing down represents the Shakti aspect of creation, and a triangle with its apex pointing up represents the Shiva aspect. Just as bindu stands for the center of consciousness, so does the triangle stand for the creative genetrix. This is the first stage in the movement outward from pure unalloyed Consciousness.

The circle in a yantra represents the cyclic and rhythmic contraction and expansion of cosmic energy. The four corners of a square represent the four directions, and thereby the totality of space. And because the entire universe is located within space, the square often appears as the base of the yantra.

Yantras are often composed of lotuses, whose petals always point out toward the circumference. In Indian mythology the lotus is associated with creation: Brahma the creator is born from the lotus. In the system of yantras, the lotus represents the power that unfolds the universe. The outward-pointing petals represent the "outpetaling" of spiritual awareness. The lotus also symbolizes the art of healthy, balanced living: because the lotus grows in the mud and yet blossoms above the water, it is a symbol of how to live in the world while remaining unaffected by it.

Seed mantras, when inscribed on yantras, represent both the visual and the auditory forms of the eternal and imperceptible vibratory ripples of divine energy contained in the yantra. The exact placement of the seed mantras helps an aspirant to locate those precise vibrations of divine energy in his own body, for according to yogis there is a perfect equation between a yantra and the human body. Thus, all the different components of yantra—bindus, triangles, circles, squares, lotuses, and seed mantras—represent different aspects of primordial energy that evolve into and govern both macrocosm and microcosm.

At another level, yantras and the energy contained in them represent the gods and goddesses who are elaborately described in Tantric literature. That is, Tantric mythology is a visually oriented explanation of yantra.

Deities

Deities are the personified form of the subtle forces of creation. When we shift our attention from an abstract and geometrical representation of the divine energy to a more personified and mythological one, a yantra turns into a deity.

Personality traits, philosophical convictions, and, most importantly, subtle impressions of previous spiritual practices cause meditators to experience the same truth differently. In one case, truth is revealed in the form of a mantra or yantra. In another, truth may reveal itself in the form of a deity. However, the principle behind the revelation of truth in any of these forms is the same. Those who are trained in Western science and psychology tend to have a greater affinity with yantras and mandalas than with personified forms of deities because their minds are at greater ease with an abstract form of the Divine. On the other hand, the abstract lines of yantras fail to quench the devotional thirst of those with a religious bent, especially those who are not acquainted with the language of symbols. Sometimes even people whose intellect is dominant feel the need for a personal relationship with the Divine, feeling intuitively that repeating or meditating on a sacred sound will invoke God in an actual form. Intuition fosters anticipation, and anticipation creates its own reality—this is the ground on which the power of mantra assumes a personified form, and a faithful practitioner is eventually rewarded by seeing the unseen.

The following stories illustrate this principle. They give us an idea of what it takes to experience the full effect of a mantra, how from mantra shakti an anthropomorphic form emerges, and how—either directly from mantra shakti or from the personified form of the divine force—a yantra may emerge.

God Emerging from Mantra

Madhusudhana Sarasvati, a monk ordained in the tradition of Shankaracharya in the sixteenth century, was both a learned scholar and a sincere seeker. He is still remembered for works such as the *Advaita Siddhi* and a commentary on the *Bhagavad Gita,* and because of this he is a vital link in the long chain of the Shankaracharya tradition. Philosophically, he was a staunch adherent of nondualism, but in his heart he was a devotee of

Lord Krishna and he longed for a spiritual experience that would bring him closer to God in the form of Krishna.

For years he privately meditated without success on a mantra said to provide the experience he was seeking. Then one night he dreamed that the only way he would attain this experience was to go to the city of Benares, where he would receive proper initiation from a master.

And so, as directed in his dream, he moved to Benares. There a mysterious saint, known to few in the city, came forward and graciously offered his guidance. But before accepting it, Madhusudhana explained, "I'm practicing sincerely. I follow all the disciplines precisely as described in the scriptures. I have repeated the mantra many more times than is required to experience the visual form of Krishna. Please tell me where I am making a mistake."

The saint responded, "My son, your philosophy is a barrier between you and this experience. You write books and give discourses in which you advocate the idea of an absolute truth that transcends all names and forms. But privately you do japa with the anticipation of seeing God face to face. The devotional part of you is asking your mantra shakti to fulfill your emotional needs, but your intellect is undermining this request. Your devotional fervor is creating intellectual confusion, and the force of your intellect is creating emotional instability. Only when you overcome this problem will you rejoice in the blissful experience of mantra shakti at various levels. The grace of God is already with you. All you need is the final touch and you will be there."

So saying, the saint uttered the same mantra Madhusudhana had been practicing for so long and bestowed his blessing, imparting as well clear, systematic instructions for meditating on the mantra and undertaking contemplative practices. Finally he instructed Madhusudhana to move to Vrindavan, the land of Krishna's childhood, where he would receive the consummate experience.

Moving on to Vrindavan, Madhusudhana undertook his practice sincerely and wholeheartedly. As the saint had predicted, one day the mantra shakti materialized in the form of Lord Krishna and emerged in the world composed of Madhusudhana's thoughts, feelings, love, faith, and devotion *(bhava jagat)*. Madhusudhana was thrilled. Lover and beloved, meditator and object of meditation met, and the delight of both culminated in the experience of oneness between the two. The personified mantra shakti then subsided in Madhusudhana, and he assimilated the fully awakened mantra shakti.

Madhusudhana was fully prepared to meet the anthropomorphic form of the mantra shakti; his intellect was clear, and the force of his emotions completely stilled. Long before the mantra shakti materialized in the form of Krishna, Madhusudhana knew that there is only one reality, that this reality is transcendental, and that his mind was requesting the mantra shakti to assume the form of Krishna because of his *samskaras*. The omniscient mantra shakti was aware of Madhusudhana's desires and his need to have them fulfilled, and that is why the experience of the highest came to Madhusudhana in this manner.

YANTRA EMERGING FROM MANTRA

This story will shed some light on the complex process by which mantra shakti materializes in a personified form, and at the same time it illustrates the relationships among mantra, deity, and yantra. It provides insight into how previous karmic residues can interfere with the condensation of mantra shakti, and shows as well how an untimely experience may evoke negative *samskaras*.

Vidyaranya, a renunciate in the tradition of Shankaracharya, lived in the Vijaya Nagaram empire in the fourteenth century. His fame was great and his honors many. In addition to serving as the empire's prime minister, he held the position of *raja guru* (the spiritual preceptor of the royal family). Vidyaranya was also one of the most learned scholars of his day. He wrote numerous books on Vedanta and organized a group of scholars to restore, copy, edit, and write commentaries on Vedic scriptures.

In his private life Vidyaranya was a devout practitioner of the *gayatri* mantra. He began practicing this mantra at an early age and intensified his practice as time went on. By the time he reached his seventies, his spiritual yearning had become so intense that even though he was highly respected, he became profoundly dissatisfied with his achievements, his knowledge, and the amount of energy he was putting into his practice. And so, throwing aside all other duties, obligations, and commitments, he poured his entire mind and heart into meditation on the *gayatri* mantra. As the years passed and the direct experience of mantra shakti did not manifest, his dissatisfaction and frustration grew.

Finally, when he was in his nineties, he was overcome by dejection. One day he simply walked away from his house and wandered through the streets of the city, paying no attention to where he was going or why. He ended up in the outskirts, where he found himself drawn to a desolate area used as a cremation ground.

As he wandered across the charnel ground, a rough-looking stranger suddenly appeared and addressed him in an authoritative tone: "What seems to be the trouble, learned teacher?"

No one had ever spoken to him like this, but because the man seemed to be at peace with himself, Vidyaranya overcame the alarm he felt from the desolation of his surroundings and the forceful personality of this strange man and humbly replied, "Kindly accept my homage. Surely you are someone beyond my comprehension. Please unveil your true identity and help me overcome the misery in which my soul is drowning."

The mysterious man replied, "Know me to be a resident of the cremation grounds. Destruction is creation for me. Ugliness enhances my eternal beauty. That's all you need to know about me. As for you, you have no reason to be impatient. The knower that dwells within you knows what is best for you, when it should be granted, where, and how."

Realizing this extraordinary man was a mystic, Vidyaranya said, "Please tell me, why doesn't my practice bear fruit?"

The mystic replied, "Your previous karmas are impeding the ripening of the fruits of your practice."

"Even after such a prolonged and intense practice, won't my karmas leave me alone?"

The saint smiled and said, "You were born in a scholarly and priestly family where repeating the *gayatri* mantra is a custom. Without going through the process of being a student, you became a teacher. You did not allow yourself to receive the guidance and blessings of a teacher and a tradition. Nevertheless, whatever practice you have done on your own has its merit. Look behind you. Do you see those seven piles of fire? The first six are almost reduced to ash, but the seventh—the one farthest in the distance—is still burning."

Vidyaranya looked behind him and nodded.

The saint continued, "These seven piles of fire represent seven of your past lives. The karmas accumulated in six of these lifetimes have been consumed, but the fire of knowledge generated by the shakti of the *gayatri* mantra has not yet consumed the karmas in the seventh pile. Therefore, continue your practice. When the time is right you will attain the final experience."

A long conversation ensued, during which Vidyaranya pleaded that he was old and must attain the experience before his body fell apart. He begged the mystic to initiate him and grant the experience, without making him wait any longer. The mystic refused, patiently explaining that there is a difference between undertaking a mantra practice as part of a family custom and doing the practice systematically with pure spiritual fervor. He emphasized the importance of remaining under the supervision of a competent master while committing oneself to an intense practice. He spoke about the power of *samskaras* and explained why it was not appropriate for Vidyaranya to gain the direct experience of mantra shakti so soon. But Vidyaranya would not listen. He kept insisting that he could not wait, and pleaded with the mystic to grant him the experience he had been longing for.

Seeing the hand of providence in Vidyaranya's insistence, the mystic finally relented. Repeating the *gayatri* mantra, he bestowed the highest initiation—*shaktipata*—and told Vidyaranya to sit down and repeat the mantra. When he did so the first time, the mantra shakti appeared in front of him in her full glory. Vidyaranya was simultaneously delighted and enraged. "What kind of mother are you that you ignore your child and come to his rescue only when he is old?" he shouted. "You merciless stone-hearted mother! May you turn into stone and stay at this cremation ground!"

To Vidyaranya's horror, the personified mantra shakti instantly turned to stone. Realizing what he had done, he fell at the feet of the mystic.

The saint looked at him lovingly and said, "I told you. But it doesn't matter. Don't live in the past. Stay here and attend Her for the rest of your life. I hope you will come to understand and assimilate the mystery behind what has happened here, and that through your experience seekers in the future will understand and remember this lesson."

To the average person, the statue at the cremation ground would appear to be inert, no different from many other emblems, statues, and idols used in religious observances. But to Vidyaranya it was the embodied mantra shakti—the fruit of his lifelong practice in visible form. To him it was not an idol, but the Divine Mother Herself. Bound by the power of his words, "May you turn into stone and stay at this cremation ground," the Mother stayed, and so did the son.

Several years passed, and Vidyaranya realized that his body had become so fragile that it was time to give it back to the dust. He looked at the Divine Mother and sadly inquired, "Who will tend you, O Mother? Hardly anyone in the world knows who you are." Instantly, the essence of mantra shakti emerged from the stone and turned into a yantra. Vidyaranya understood what this meant, and with reverence he picked it up and held it to his heart. Then he called his students, the emperors of Vijaya Nagaram, and gave them the yantra along with instructions as to how it was to be treated. For several generations it was tended by the members of the royal family. Eventually divine providence maneuvered events so that the yantra reached one of the Shankaracharya monasteries, where it is still tended by an adept assigned by the tradition.

It is evident from Vidyaranya's writings that he understood the law of karma and its effect on spiritual practices, but driven by his impatience, he disregarded that knowledge as well as the advice of the mystic. This story shows how impatience veils our intellect, causing us to forget even those principles we know well. That is why it is said that patience is required to keep us on the path and to expand the field of our perception so that we come to regard a decade as if it were a week.

In the course of mantra *sadhana,* there is no standard rule or procedure for gaining a particular spiritual experience in a particular manner. In the case of Madhusudhana, his *sam-skaras* and his strong desire were at least partially behind the materialization of mantra shakti into a personified form. Likewise, Vidyaranya's intense longing touched the heart of the mantra shakti and later, complying with Vidyaranya's determination that it be properly attended, the mantra shakti materialized in the form of a yantra.

MISCONCEPTIONS ABOUT YANTRAS

The theory underlying the relationships among mantra, deity, and yantra—even though it is perfectly sound, systematic, and convincing—addresses only a few of the general characteristics; the theory can never convey the precise and subtle dynamics of these relationships. A vision of a yantra or a personified form of mantra shakti is only one of the many signs and symptoms of progress in mantra *sadhana,* and it is usually the culmination of prolonged and intense practice. For example, before Vidyaranya envisioned the material form of *gayatri* shakti, the process of inner purification and transformation had been long underway. Symbolically, six piles of his karmic impurities had been reduced to ash, and the last was still being consumed. As the sage advised, it would have been better for him to wait until the seventh pile was also consumed before asking to meet the Divine Mother face to face.

Materialization of mantra shakti into a deity or yantra is not the ultimate goal of mantra *sadhana;* in fact, such occurrences are extremely rare. Further, visions of deities or mystical experiences with yantras do not necessarily induce a long-lasting, qualitative change in our personality. Often when people have such visions, the effects soon fade. These experiences generate a surge of faith and devotion, but soon, under the influence of mundane reality, the *samskaras* reassert themselves and these so-called visionaries revert to their old selves. With the passage of time, they may not even know whether the experience really took place. Visionary experiences provide a lasting push in a constructive direction only to those whose minds and hearts are purified, whose senses and nervous systems are balanced, and who understand the correlation between mantra shakti and its yantric or personified form.

Those who are not adequately prepared have a tendency to superimpose their own interpretations on the experience and to overemphasize its value—a tendency which leads them to believe that they have made great progress or even that they have attained mastery. They no longer focus on their practice, but instead busy themselves telling all they meet about the greatness of their experience and lauding the teacher or tradition that introduced them to the practice. Others completely misinterpret such experiences, become frightened, and drop their practices altogether.

It is not constructive to become overly fascinated with mantra, yantra, and deities, reading miraculous stories about them, and searching for a practice that will yield such experiences. Those who find such a practice soon discover that it is infused with anxiety and anticipation. This may cause them to hallucinate, especially if their nervous systems have been weakened by drug use or an unhealthy lifestyle. The colors and forms they may see during their meditation are highly questionable.

Because mantras consist of vibratory sound patterns, logically they all should have a corresponding visual form. In other words, in theory each mantra should have a yantra—but in reality this is not the case. There are many more mantras than there are yantras. In fact, many mantras have a single yantra in common. This is one reason why, no matter how much intellectual energy we invest in this subject, it is never fully satisfactory. In fact, it is often misunderstood. For example, most teachers who prescribe a yantra to accompany the practice of mantra are not working with yantras which have emerged from the vibration of mantra. Rather, they are using yantras they have seen drawn on a piece of paper, cloth, or bark, or inscribed on metal or wood.

Furthermore, students often learn the spiritual significance of a yantra from teachers or books by studying the symbolic meaning of its dot, triangles, squares, petals, and circles. But not every yantra has all of these components. Some consist of only a triangle, others a circle, others more than one triangle or circle, and others a combination of several of these elements. Also, some aspirants are under the impression that the practice of yantra facilitates the process of mantra meditation; they believe they do not need to wait for the exact shape of yantra to emerge directly from the mantra shakti in order to use it later as an object for meditation. These days yantras are mass-produced and can even be purchased by mail. Some people use such yantras as objects of concentration; others keep them on their altars, believing they will emit a spiritual vibration; still others use them as mere decoration. The truth is, however, that only an awakened yantra has power.

Yantras drawn on paper or inscribed on metal or stone have no value unless their latent shakti has been awakened by someone who is already awakened and who knows how to awaken others. Such an adept does not usually rely on such yantras. As mentioned before, there is a perfect equation between each yantra and the human body, and one who has gained the experience of oneness between his body and the yantra can literally produce a yantra from his body at will. Yantras emerging from the body of an adept are called self-born (*svayam-bhuva*) yantras. A fully realized master gives his student such a self-born yantra or a yantra that the tradition has kept awake. Or he may simply initiate an aspirant into mantra *sadhana* and let the practice generate whatever experience is best. Unlike yogis, Sanskrit scholars with priestly knowledge often attempt to invoke and localize the divine shakti along the lines of yantra. To accomplish this, they perform a long and elaborate ritual described in the scriptures, called *prana pratishtha*. To an aspirant in the yogic tradition, however, who has been initiated by an adept master, these yantras are of little or no value, for such a student knows that the most complete yantra is the human body itself.

THE UNIVERSE IN MINIATURE

According to yoga science, the human body is a miniature universe—anything that exists in the universe also exists in the human body. This is a fundamental and universal law of yogic metaphysics and spirituality, one that has been intuitively experienced by the yogis and verified by their experiments throughout the millennia. All branches of science developed in the East—Ayurveda, physics, chemistry, alchemy, metallurgy, astronomy, and so on—are grounded in this one spiritual experience: there is a perfect equation between the human body and the universe. All mantras, yantras, deities, mandalas, temples, mosques, churches, holy shrines, and other spiritual forces exist in the human body. This may sound like a radical statement, and it may be inconceivable intellectually, but it is an experiential fact.

The vast literature of yoga describes this equation as well as the correlation between the human body and mantras. They also undertake the task of explaining the correlation between mantra and yantra. For example, the scriptures belonging to the *maha vidyas*, kundalini yoga, and Tantra expound upon the hierarchies of the divine force which dwells in different centers in the human body, along with the vibratory patterns that correspond to different phonemes composing the articulate form of mantras.

Just as there are countless currents of energy in the cosmos, all of which are distinct from each other, so are there countless energy currents in the human body. In yogic literature these are called *nadis*. Of the 72,000 distinct *nadis* the yogis have identified, fourteen are of principal importance. Yogis have also discovered the exact nature of these major energy currents, their pathways in the body, how they interact with other energy currents, and what effect they have on the body, nervous system, biochemistry, and mind. Then, realizing that it is practically impossible to enunciate distinctly the sound that is produced from the vibrations of each *nadi,* yogis with extraordinary spiritual powers captured the entire range of sound produced by all these energy currents, and divided them into forty-eight parts. That is how the forty-eight letters of the Sanskrit alphabet were discovered.

The yogis have also discovered that every letter of the Sanskrit alphabet has its own color, shape, presiding force, and unique transformative quality, as well as its own seer. They have also experienced the relationship between these letters and different planets, stars, and constellations. They have discovered the approximate location of these letters in the human body and the particular pranic or psychological forces to which they correspond. The chart on page 155 (Figure 1) gives the locations of the letters at the superficial level of the human body.

At a more subtle level, the Sanskrit phonemes relate to the energy currents which lie deep within the interior of the human body. Each of the 72,000 currents has a distinct sound, although they are too diffuse and vague to be enunciated distinctly. Moreover, the yogis have identified places in the body where two or more energy currents cross. In mantra *shastra,* the point where two energy currents intersect is called a *sandhi,* the point where three energy currents cross is called *marma shthana,* and the point where more than three energy currents converge is called a *chakra.* Here at the chakras, the vibratory patterns of energy are strong and vibrant. At the center of each chakra a distinct sound predominates, and other distinct sounds are centered around it. That is why, in kundalini yoga, each chakra is represented as having a particular letter at its center, as well as a letter on each petal. The location of the seven chief chakras described in kundalini yoga and the sounds corresponding to each are illustrated in Figure 2 on pages 156–58.

All yantras—from the simplest to the most complex—are external representations of the chakras. Most of them correspond to one chakra or, at most, a few chakras in the body. However, there is one yantra, and only one, that includes all the chakras. That is Sri Yantra—the yantra of the *maha vidya* variously known as Sodashi, Sri Vidya, or Tripura (see Figure 3, page 159). Further, all yantras are found in Sri Yantra. Sri Yantra encompasses not only the seven chakras described in kundalini yoga, but many other yantras, both prominent and minor, described in other schools of yoga. For example, Figures 4A–C on pages 160–62 illustrate the correlation between nine circuits of Sri Yantra and nine of the principal chakras in the human body. The scriptures explain how to use Sri Yantra to identify within the body all the different parts of the cosmos as well as the elements found on the Earth.

SOME TIPS ON PRACTICE

Put in the context of yantra, kundalini, and chakras, the science of mantra becomes quite complex, and its practice extremely demanding. The best way to begin to grasp these complexities and to develop the capacity to do the advanced practices is to meditate on an awakened mantra regularly and wholeheartedly. We can be confident that a mantra is awakened when we receive it from a teacher who has been initiated in the long chain of a spiritual tradition. Receiving a mantra from such a teacher also gives us the security of knowing that the guiding force of the lineage is with us. Incorporating the practice of yantra into our meditation is advisable only if we receive clear instructions from an experienced teacher and fully understand the deeper symbolic meaning of the yantra.

The intense practices of mantra *sadhana* involve a precise regimen which may include specific dietary observances, specific exercises, pranayama, living in solitude, maintaining silence, and most important, keeping a good grip on one's thoughts and emotions. During such practices it is advisable to follow the teacher's instructions accurately. Intense practice means you are already in high gear. Do not allow your impatience to push you to exceed the limit. Follow all the precautions laid out for any practice you have been given. My own experience of trying to exceed the limit illustrates this point.

I had been Sri Swami Rama's sincere student for a long time, and had been constantly asking Swamiji to initiate me into the higher practices of yoga. Finally he said, "Sonny, the kind of practice you are requesting requires a firm sitting posture. The actual practice can begin only after you have worked with the *muladhara* center. Do japa of such and such mantra and pay attention to what I am saying."

Swamiji explained the significance of the mantra and described the observances that accompany the practice, telling me to complete a certain number of repetitions of the mantra in thirty-three days. I started the practice, but because of either carelessness or a lack of strong determination, I failed

THE SANSKRIT ALPHABET

अ	forehead	ञ	tip of the fingers, left hand
आ	face	ट	right hip joint
इ	right eye	ठ	right knee
ई	left eye	ड	right ankle
उ	right ear	ढ	root of the toes, right foot
ऊ	left ear	ण	tip of the toes, right foot
ऋ	right nostril	त	left hip joint
ॠ	left nostril	थ	left knee
ऌ	right cheek	द	left ankle
ॡ	left cheek	ध	root of the toes, left foot
ए	upper lip	न	tip of the toes, left foot
ऐ	lower lip	प	right side of the torso
ओ	upper teeth	फ	left side of the torso
औ	lower teeth	ब	back
अं	crown of head	भ	navel
अः	mouth	म	stomach
क	right shoulder joint	य	heart
ख	right elbow	र	top of right shoulder
ग	right wrist	ल	between shoulder blades, just under neck
घ	root of the fingers, right hand	व	top of left shoulder
ङ	tip of the fingers, right hand	श	area from heart to right hand
च	left shoulder joint	ष	area from heart to left hand
छ	left elbow	स	area from heart to right toes
ज	left wrist	ह	area from heart to left toes
झ	root of the fingers, left hand	ळ	from heart to orbit of face
		क्ष	from heart to abdomen

Figure 1

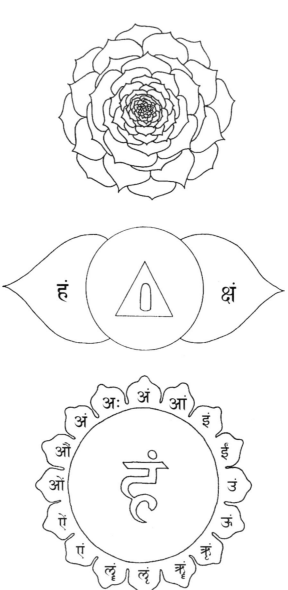

Figure 2A

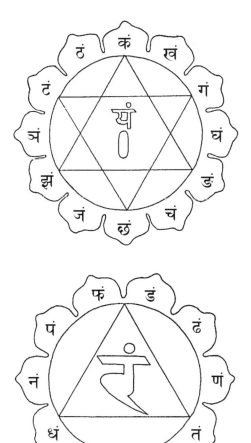

Figure 2B

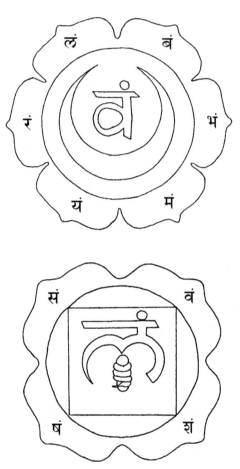

Figure 2C

SRI YANTRA

Figure 3

C H A K R A S   S R I   Y A N T R A

SAHASRARA CHAKRA

NINTH CIRCUIT:
Bliss

●

TRIKUTI CHAKRA

EIGHTH CIRCUIT:
*The Giver of all
Accomplishments*

BHRIKUTI CHAKRA

SEVENTH CIRCUIT:
Remover of all Illnesses

Figure 4A

AJNA CHAKRA

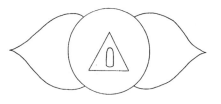

SIXTH CIRCUIT:
Protector of All

VISHUDDHA CHAKRA

FIFTH CIRCUIT:
Accomplisher of All Purposes

ANAHATA CHAKRA

FOURTH CIRCUIT:
The Giver of All Auspiciousness

Figure 4B

MANIPURA CHAKRA

THIRD CIRCUIT:
Protector of All

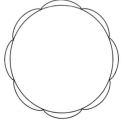

SVADHISHTHANA CHAKRA

SECOND CIRCUIT:
The Fulfiller of All Expectations

MULADHARA CHAKRA

FIRST CIRCUIT:
Enchanter of the Triple Words

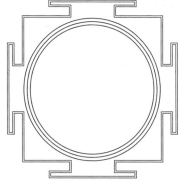

Figure 4C

to follow the observances strictly. Realizing my mistake, I started the practice again with renewed determination. This time I followed all the observances longer, but I still broke them before completing the practice. This happened again and again. With each failure my resolution became stronger, but it was still not strong enough to get me through the entire thirty-three days. Finally I was so frustrated that I decided to get the whole practice done, no matter what. If I did the practice intensely, I thought, it would take less time, and I would run a smaller risk of violating the observances. So I decided to triple the daily repetitions of the mantra in order to complete the practice in eleven days.

It was winter and Swamiji was in India, so there was no way to seek his guidance or to ask his permission to intensify the practice, but I did tell his secretary that I wished to go into silence for a short time. That evening Swamiji called from India and his secretary told him what I had said. He was quiet for a few minutes, and then said, "Give him my cottage, and make sure no one disturbs him. Once a day someone should give him food. He can keep milk and fruit in the refrigerator to use as he feels the need."

I moved to Swamiji's cottage and began my practice. Completing it in eleven days required sitting more than twelve hours each day, and this was very tiring. There were times when my mind refused to cooperate. Yet, with God's grace, my own strong determination, and the ability to tolerate physical discomfort, I completed the practice. I was exhausted. As soon as it was finished, I sat down on the couch and immediately fell asleep.

In a dream- or reverie-like state, someone came to me, someone I was sure was a great soul. He sat down and said lovingly, "I am very glad that you completed the practice this time." Then he closed his eyes and was silent.

I was overjoyed by the comment. But then the saint gently opened his eyes and said with a smile, "Do you see the seed on my palm? You know you sow this seed in the soil. When conditions are favorable, the seed sprouts. In a certain period of time it consumes a certain amount of water, heat, light, and nutrients; then it blossoms and gives fruit. Now tell me, what will happen if you provide all that water, heat, and light at once? This is a powerful and healthy seed, fully equipped with all the potential for turning into a tree. Too intense heat and too much food in too little time . . . poor beautiful seed."

So saying, the saint disappeared, or the dream vanished. I was happy, but I was also sad. I got the lesson. Like the outer world, the inner world has its own rules and laws, and, especially at the more advanced stages, we must listen to those who are residents of the inner realm. Intellectual sharpness is helpful, but faith—the virtue of an innocent heart—is indispensable. The two together yield the patience and the skill to interpret properly the subtle instructions of the teacher and the scriptures and to act accordingly.

My cosmic and all-pervasive form

is invisible to your ordinary eyes.

Therefore I grant you the divine

eye—intuitive vision—so you

may behold my yogic and godly

glory.

Bhagavad Gita 11:8

SHAKTIPATA: THE DESCENT OF GRACE

Shaktipata is one of the most exciting concepts in the vast literature of yoga. That a master can transmit her spiritual power in an instant, freeing us from the hardships of practice and discipline, is a thrilling idea indeed. The problem is that many spiritual seekers think of shaktipata as a kind of instant lottery, and desiring to win, they often shift their attention away from practicing mantra meditation and cultivating an understanding of spirituality in the hope of finding someone who will bestow enlightenment with a touch. This reflects the widespread misunderstanding of what shaktipata initiation is all about.

The word *shaktipata* means "bestowing energy, or lighting the lamp." It can be quite different from mantra initiation, however, for after mantra initiation mantra shakti unfolds its transformative power gradually as the student practices—each level of unfoldment and assimilation becomes the ground for the next. The pace of inner illumination is so natural and so gradual that we may not always be aware that it is taking place. But with certain kinds of shaktipata initiation, a level of energy the student has never before experienced is transmitted in an instant. And if the flow of energy is strong, the student is both startled and thrilled.

Shaktipata is the process by which a master leads prepared students to higher levels of consciousness. As a result they gain a firsthand experience of the inner truth, and in the light of this the trivial concerns of lower reality lose their binding power. The student becomes fearless and selfless, realizing that he is under divine protection. All obstacles turn into means. Such is the fruit of shaktipata.

Just as there are several levels of mantra initiation, so are there various levels and forms of shaktipata, some mild, others intense. Mild shaktipata gives the student a gentle push in the direction of spiritual unfoldment that may manifest simply as an increase in faith and determination and a decrease in sloth and doubt. A slightly more intense form of shaktipata may unleash a stream of inner joy, creating an environment that enables the mind to become one-pointed during meditation so that the mantra flows effortlessly. With the transmission of intense shaktipata the student reaches the state of *samadhi* and experiences the oneness of mantra, *ishta deva, gurudeva,* and himself. As we shall see, all degrees of shaktipata may either come through a living teacher or flow directly from the grace of God.

Shaktipata is a transmission of spiritual energy from a master to a qualified and fully prepared student. It is neither an accidental event nor part of a formal, scheduled ceremony. The shaktipata initiation that Sri Swami Rama received from his master is a case in point.

Swamiji was trained from an early age; he spent years practicing meditation and other spiritual disciplines under his master's guidance, while studying the scriptures and learning from other adepts as well. He knew that his master was a great yogi and mystic, and he often saw adept practitioners visiting his master and receiving instructions from him.

After seventeen years of sincere and regular practice, Swamiji still had not attained a direct experience of Truth. After a long debate with himself, he decided to ask his master to bestow shaktipata on him, for he felt there was no other way to reach the goal. So he went to his master and said in a humble but firm voice, "For so long now I have been closing my eyes in meditation, and I end up with nothing but a headache. I have wasted my time, and I find little joy in life. I have worked hard and sincerely. You said that it would take fourteen years, and this is my seventeenth year of practice. I did everything that you told me to do. I am tired of life. If you do not do shaktipata for me, I will jump into the Ganges and drown."

His master expressed no concern for him. Instead, he asked, "Are you sure you have been practicing sincerely and wholeheartedly? Have you been following my teachings? Did I ever teach you to commit suicide? When do you want to drown yourself?"

Swamiji had reached a point at which life without the spiritual ecstasy he was longing for held no further attraction. He replied, "Right now! I gave up everything. I'm of no use to the world; I'm of no use to you." With that he got up and walked toward the Ganges.

Swamiji's disappointment and dejection increased when his master told him, "You know how to swim. You'd better weight yourself down with rocks so that you can drown easily."

With renewed determination Swamiji bowed his head, and saying goodbye to his master, he went to the Ganges and tied some big rocks around his waist. Then, when his master saw that Swamiji was fully determined to jump, he called, "Wait! Sit down there. In one minute I will give you *samadhi.*"

Although Swamiji did not know if his master really meant it, he thought it was worth waiting a minute to see. So he sat down in his meditative pose. His master came and touched his forehead. Immediately all thought constructs vanished. His consciousness turned inward and became so absorbed in the deepest level of his being that he no longer remembered that he had a body. As he writes in *Living with the Himalayan Masters*, Swamiji remained in that blissful state for nine hours, but the effect was long-lasting. In addition to experiencing an unconditional inner bliss, he attained a state of fearlessness and selflessness, and he began to understand life properly.

Later Swamiji asked his master, "How did that experience descend? Was it due to your effort or my effort? And why, after all these years, did it happen when I was in such a desperate state of mind?"

His master replied, "It was grace. When a human being becomes exhausted after making all possible sincere efforts, and cries out in despair, the highest state of devotion emerges. And during that spontaneous devotional flood, the student attains ecstasy. That is called the grace of God. In a sense this grace is unconditional, but it is still the fruit of faithful and sincere effort. You had pursued your practice faithfully, and the subtlest obstacle was removed by that 'final touch.' Shaktipata is the twilight in which self-effort ends and grace dawns."

The spiritual energy transmitted from master to student has its source in God. A teacher in human form is simply a vehicle for that transmission, and only after releasing her own self-identity into the perennial stream of guru shakti can she become an instrument in the hands of the Divine and light the lamps of others. But she will do only that which is determined by the Divine. There is no way God can make a mistake, either by bestowing grace or by blocking it. God whispers silently in the heart of the master, who then spontaneously transmits shaktipata to the prepared student.

WHEN SHAKTIPATA IS NOT SHAKTIPATA

When a teacher gives in to a student's demand to receive shaktipata, an unpleasant experience is bound to result. A teacher working under the guidance of her master and other sages of the lineage will not make such a mistake, but a teacher who falls under the influence of ego may show off and say, "Tomorrow I will give you shaktipata. Then you will know who I am and how great my master is." With the power of her determination *(sankalpa shakti)* such a teacher may be able to awaken the dormant shakti within the student, but she creates a problem for herself, because by doing so she goes against the divine will. Such behavior simply feeds her ego and makes her selfish and hypocritical, and she will soon fall from grace.

When a teacher exerts her concentrated psychic powers indiscriminately over devoted students who are not prepared, the students are not able to assimilate the transmitted energy. Uncontrollable emotional fits of crying, laughing, singing, and dancing can result—even a nervous breakdown. Such displays have little or no spiritual value. Emotion properly channeled may help love and devotion unfold, but when strong emotions are stirred up which cannot be properly assimilated, damage can result. Some students may become spacey and apathetic. Those with subtle mental impurities may become egotistical and destructive. Fortunately, the effects of this kind of shaktipata do not last long. The allure of such teachers and their teachings evaporates, and most students move on to the next level of their search.

However, such occurrences raise a series of questions: Is it shaktipata if it comes from a teacher's ego instead of from the Primordial Master? How can a teacher operate under the sway of ego if she is connected to the divine will? If a teacher's ego is uncontrolled and she has a strong desire to impress students with her power, how can she bestow spiritual power? If it is not real spiritual power, is it shaktipata?

The answers are clear. It is not shaktipata but "ego-pata" if it does not come from the Primordial Master. Through practice and God's grace, a teacher may gain spiritual power and afterwards, under the influence of ignorance and ego, may disconnect herself from the Source and begin to act independently.

There are many instances of this throughout history. Ravana in Indian literature and Lucifer in Christian literature are examples of spiritually evolved beings who fell from grace yet retained the power to attract followers. But as long as a teacher remains connected to the divine will, she cannot make a mistake by conferring shaktipata on someone who is not ready, or by refusing shaktipata to someone destined for it. Love and compassion, accompanied with wisdom, flow effortlessly and spontaneously from such a teacher. A teacher who is not connected to the Source but is acting by her own whim may be able to bestow a mild degree of spiritual energy. But because it is contaminated by ego, it will have an adverse effect on the student's psyche. This kind of transmission is not shaktipata.

Maha Diksha and *Krama Diksha*

According to the scriptures, there are many different kinds of shaktipata. All of them fall into two major categories: *maha diksha* (the highest level of initiation) and *krama diksha* (step-by-step initiation).

Maha diksha is the rarest form of shaktipata. Here spiritual energy is transmitted in its full brilliance, through an adept, to a perfectly prepared aspirant. *Maha diksha* is the means by which the master removes those subtle obstacles which are virtually impossible to eradicate by any other means. From this kind of shaktipata a student spontaneously reaches a state beyond mind called *unmana*—a state of awareness in which no thought constructs or modifications remain in the mind. The mind becomes an integral part of Pure Consciousness and no longer stands as a wall between the individual and universal being. The aspirant and Shiva—Universal Consciousness—become one. The yogi experiences pure existence, consciousness, and bliss as his intrinsic nature. Yoga texts call this state *nirvikalpa samadhi*. In the Upanishads it is called *turiya* (the fourth state, that transcends waking, dreaming, and deep sleep).

According to a prominent scripture, *Saundaryalahari*, the master confers *maha diksha* only after the student has completed a full course of mantra japa, which has cut most of the student's karmic knots and loosened even the subtlest ones. Then *maha diksha* descends through the master. As a result, kundalini shakti awakens and travels upward, cutting asunder the three main knots: *rudra granthi*, *vishnu granthi*, and *brahma granthi*.

Granthi means "knot, or entanglement." The knot created by the entanglements of tamasic karmas are destroyed as the fire at the navel center is ignited and fanned. The scriptures refer to this as breaking the knot of *rudra granthi*. Similarly, the power released by *maha diksha* frees the aspirant from the binding powers of sattvic and rajasic karmas at the heart center *(vishnu granthi)* and at the center between the eyebrows *(brahma granthi)*. The aspirant so blessed experiences the unfoldment of an infinite potential within, as kundalini shakti passes through the six lower chakras and enters the *brahma nadi*, the channel leading to the seventh and highest chakra, the *sahasrara*. The entrance to the *brahma nadi* is known as *bindu*, and the process of entering the bindu is called *bindu bhedana*. The force that enables the process is called *anugraha shakti* (grace).

This highest of shaktipatas is given by a master to a student in its totality only if that student is perfectly fit physically, emotionally, and intellectually, and it is conferred only on one who is expected to be the custodian of the lineage. At that moment the aspirant gains the experience of fourfold union: mantra, its presiding force, the master, and the aspirant's self merge into one. It is a complete awakening.

By contrast, *krama diksha* is a process of gradual unfoldment of the inner shakti. The word *krama* means "sequence," and in this context it means "step-by-step shaktipata." Here a small amount of energy is transmitted at a time; when that energy is assimilated, the student is ready for the next step. Each step of the process becomes the ground for the following steps.

Practically speaking, *krama diksha* begins with mantra initiation. In a living tradition of yoga science, a master imparts her blessings in proportion to the capacity and preparedness of the student. The guru mantra is the first step and is the foundation on which the aspirant's entire spiritual practice rests. From time to time the teacher may initiate the student into a variety of other practices, permitting spiritual energy to flow from the Source and illuminate the inner realm in the exact measure that a student can assimilate. According to the scriptures this energy descends in waves of gradually increasing intensity, and with each wave some karmas are destroyed and some obstacles disintegrate.

Krama diksha is an ongoing process of *sadhana* rather than a particular event. The different stages of this process bring about a qualitative change in our personality, and as these changes take place, both student and teacher spontaneously understand that one level of inner illumination has been reached. Whatever method the teacher uses for transmitting the next step is a form of *krama diksha;* this process continues to deepen and change as the student's ability to assimilate it increases. The surest sign of *krama diksha* is the natural unfoldment of clarity of mind and inner inspiration.

EVIDENCE OF SHAKTIPATA

As *krama diksha* unfolds we see the contrast between ordinary reality and higher reality, and as a result the mind is spontaneously free from doubts about the validity of inner reality and the existence of a higher purpose in life. We are motivated to do our practice more one-pointedly and wholeheartedly. The intensity of the experience may fade, but the memory remains, and that memory compels us to make ourselves available for another experience. But even if we do not attain that experience again after making sincere efforts, we cannot be defeated by frustration and doubt. We never drop our quest, no matter what obstacles confront us. If our constant effort becomes tiring, we pray instead of complaining. And prayer supported by the memory of the experience of shaktipata is full of spiritual yearning; it strengthens our desire for enlightenment.

Ordinarily, people do not want to experience God as much as they want to acquire worldly possessions and experiences through the grace of God. According to saints and yogis, when we long to receive the grace of God for its own sake, we have already been graced by the Divine. The desire for enlightenment and the longing to find God in this lifetime are definite signs of shaktipata.

Mantra *siddhi* is another sign of shaktipata. This is a state in which mantra flows effortlessly and continuously, day and night, because the mantra has created such a deep groove in the mind that the mind rests constantly in mantra awareness. When we attain mantra *siddhi* our dream world is filled with mantra shakti, and our mind is filled with mantra awareness when we wake up in the morning. We feel secure and protected by the Divine in every area of life. Success and failure, loss and gain have little effect on our inner equilibrium, for we know that the external world is just a thin slice of reality. The experts say that if the mantra comes forward and rescues the frightened aspect of our being when we are having a nightmare, the process of mantra *siddhi* has begun.

After shaktipata the theories and practices described in the scriptures seem to unveil their meanings by themselves. Our understanding of the scriptures matches our inner experience, and we no longer feel the need to verify the validity of our scriptural understanding or to garner others' opinions to support our knowledge. Our own knowledge is a source of inspiration and inner guidance in and of itself. This is where the domain of *krama diksha* ends. At the last phase of *krama diksha* we begin to intuitively feel the oneness between the teacher and the Primordial Master, God. We realize that the instrument—the teacher in human form—and God, who uses this instrument, are identical.

Now we enter the realm of *maha diksha*. We long to experience this oneness for ourselves. Without considering other teachers to be inferior, we are fully convinced that our teacher is Shiva himself, and as a result of this conviction an unwavering faith in the teacher unfolds. Effortlessly, we find ourselves totally surrendering to her. At this stage of conviction, faith, and self-surrender, all other relationships in the world lose their charm. The student-teacher relationship gives way to the master-disciple relationship. The teacher becomes the master. Intense longing to have a direct experience of the essence of the master is the condition under which we transcend the realm of *krama diksha* and enter the realm of *maha diksha*.

A SHAKTIPATA EXPERIENCE

The following story of a contemporary saint illustrates the descent of divine grace and the step-by-step process of transformation that followed. Not too long ago the soul who came to be named Swami Krishnananda was born in Jaunpur, a district of North India. Because he was raised in a rural area where education was virtually unknown, he did not learn to read or write. When he reached manhood he went to Bombay, where he found work as a servant in the house of a famous businessman named Jhun-jhun Wala, one of the biggest traders of silver and gold in the city. As the years passed, the young man earned the family's trust, and gradually he found an intimate place among them. He was given tasks that involved much responsibility, for he had proven himself to be sincere, honest, and reliable.

One day, as this man was carrying a large amount of gold

from the family's residence to one of their places of business, he was robbed, and every ounce of gold was taken from him. When he went back and reported the incident to the Jhun-jhun Wala family no one believed him because he was un-harmed—there was not a single scratch on his body nor any sign of fear on his face. First they implored him to confess, and when he stuck to his story, they threatened him. When that proved fruitless, they beat him. Still he insisted that he had been robbed. Finally they said, "You have been our family servant for a long time. We will not hand you over to the police immediately because we love you and care for you. Instead we are going to lock you up here. If you don't give our gold back to us, the police will take you to jail."

They locked him in a room and left him alone. For a day and a night this gentle man suffered humiliation, hunger, and thirst. He had never imagined that those he had served with such sincerity and love for years would treat him so cruelly. He was overcome with grief and self-pity, but gradually a feeling of disgust, not only toward the Jhun-jhun Wala family but also toward all worldly relationships, crept over him. Memories of his childhood and early youth fueled his disgust and disap-pointment. He began to pray, "O Lord, release me from this prison and help me walk toward Thee. This world is full of disappointment. True solace is only at Thy feet." He did not know any mantra or formal prayer, but the intensity of his plight made him rich in despondency, which soon grew into indifference, then to non-attachment to worldly objects and affairs, and finally to total surrender to the Divine.

With this, a wave of peace descended, sweeping away his grief and fear. He became tranquil. Grace illumined his deeper self, and he began thinking, "Worldly objects and relationships are short-lived. Rich and poor, those who are successful and those who are not, are equally miserable. Everyone is haunted by fear and insecurity. How blessed are those *sadhus* who have nothing to lose and nothing to gain. How fearless and happy! They have such a great wealth of joy that they are not affected by honor or insult. That is the world to which I belong. Who cares for the reward or punishment that comes from this other world?"

As this feeling became stronger, the members of the Jhun-jhun Wala family began to feel that they had been wrong to accuse this gentle man. They unlocked the door and offered their apologies. But to their surprise, their servant replied, "This is no one's fault. Driven by our personalities, we get into situations where we love or hate, agree or disagree with each other. My life in the world has ended. God bless you. I am leaving." They insisted that he stay, but after arguing with him for three days they realized that his mind and heart were somewhere else and let him go.

The young man left Bombay and walked barefoot to the holy city of Benares, where he visited ashrams and monasteries and sought the guidance of hundreds of *sadhus,* but no one would accept him as a student. Then one day while he was bathing in the Ganges an elderly member of the Jhun-jhun Wala family saw him and asked, "What are you doing here?" This man had been away from Bombay for a while and knew nothing of the robbery. When the former servant explained the situation, the elderly gentleman asked if he could help.

"I am illiterate," the young man responded. "I don't fit in any ashram or monastery. In each one I visit I have been offered a job, but no one wants to teach me. I do not understand the discourses they give, anyway. Please tell me how to find a master."

Because the elderly gentleman had a great interest in spirituality, he knew *sadhus* and swamis from many different traditions, so he advised the young man to seek out a learned master, Uria Baba, who lived in Vrindavan. Still barefoot, the young man made the journey. Uria Baba was happy to see him and told him that *bhakti* was the path best suited for him. He also said that he should be initiated by an adept of *bhakti* yoga named Hari Baba. This yogi graciously offered his guidance and helped him rise to the point at which he was fully prepared for *maha diksha*. Before this auspicious event, however, the student went back and forth between Hari Baba and Uria Baba, studying under their guidance and undergoing a variety of practices before he was ordained in the monastic order of Shankaracharya and given the name Swami Krishnananda.

I was fortunate enough to meet this man and spend some time in his presence. When I asked, "Maharaj-ji, please tell me the most blessed occasion of your spiritual life," he simply looked at me and smiled sweetly. In the language of silence, he clearly conveyed that I was asking him to describe that which is indescribable.

The knowledge that dawned while Krishnananda was held captive was a form of shaktipata from the invisible master, and the divine grace was so glorious and enlightening that it destroyed all his doubts, fears, and worries. It made him understand the world properly, and as a result he turned his face toward God. Grace gave him the guidance and courage to walk barefoot from Bombay to Benares, and from Benares to Vrindavan. It introduced him to masters like Uria Baba and Hari Baba. Because he was able to assimilate the initial push he received in that locked room, and because he was brave enough to invest and multiply it, he rose to the point at which renowned scholars, swamis, and mystics came to him with their questions, and people from all walks of life felt privileged to serve him. He did not give formal lectures, but during the course of *satsanga* (informal spiritual gatherings) profound wisdom flowed from him in language simple enough for all to understand.

MODES OF TRANSMISSION

Shaktipata is mysterious. When it happens, we are awestruck. We become an integral part of the experience—while it is occurring the "I" as such does not exist; we are not able to experience the experience objectively. Later, much of it fades, and what remains is difficult to capture in words.

Although the dynamics of shaktipata are indecipherable, the scriptures mention some of the better-known methods and processes through which spiritual energy is transmitted from master to disciple. These include touch, gazing, thought, mantra, or contact with tangible objects such as herbs, gems, mala beads, and so on.

When shaktipata is transmitted through touch, it is known

as *sparshi diksha*. The student is instantly absorbed in a state of bliss with one single touch from the master. At that instant the master is an embodiment of love, compassion, and wisdom, and the shakti intrinsic to her flows into the student. When a student and master live together, they naturally touch each other from time to time, but shaktipata does not occur in each such instance. For example, during the years that Sri Swami Rama and his master lived together, Swamiji touched his master's feet many times and his master put his hands on Swamiji's head many times, but it was only when Swamiji was in such despair about his *sadhana* that he was ready to jump into the Ganges that his master gave him *sparshi diksha*. Then, when his master touched his forehead, Swamiji was transported into an indescribable state of bliss.

Sometimes shaktipata is conferred by thought rather than by touch. Just by thinking, a master may push a stumbling block out of the student's way. This is called *manasi diksha*. In *manasi diksha* time and space are not barriers—a master can help a student who is on the other side of the globe. Sometimes students are aware of receiving this invisible and unspoken grace; at other times they simply notice that a long-standing obstacle has vanished and their practice is moving forward smoothly.

Another form of shaktipata is conferred by intense gazing. This is *chaksushi diksha*. By fixing her gaze on the student, an adept yogi can transmit spiritual energy directly into the student's mind and heart. There have also been incidents in which, instead of gazing directly at the student, the master gazed at an object. In one instance that I know of, the master gazed at a glass of water, then told the student to drink it and go home. A couple of hours later the blessing took effect, and the student, who was unfamiliar with Sanskrit, spontaneously uttered a mantra. As he did so a wave of joy emerged from the sound and swept away his ordinary consciousness. When he returned to normal awareness the mantra again flowed from his mouth, and he was swept away once more. Knowing this would happen, the master visited the student's home and found him on the floor. He covered him with a shawl and reassured the people around him, "Soon he will assimilate the experience; then he will be all right."

The scriptures also mention a kind of shaktipata, known as *nirvana diksha,* in which the master burns all of the student's karmas in an instant. As a result the student attains freedom from bondage, but drops the body immediately or soon after. *Nirvana diksha* is conferred only when the master realizes that the student's *prarabdha* karmas (active karmas that motivate us to be reborn) are finished. And by giving *nirvana diksha,* the master burns *sanchita* karmas (accumulated karmas which lie dormant in the unconscious mind) once and for all. Those who receive *nirvana diksha* have pure hearts, but have been stuck with a messy body, a scattered mind, or worldly circumstances that are not conducive to *sadhana.* The *Tantraloka* describes an even more startling form of shaktipata, known as *mritoddhari diksha,* which is conferred after the student is dead.

There are also instances of grace descending by itself, as the result of intense longing, intense devotion, and self-surrender. The experience of Swami Rama Tirtha at the end of the nineteenth century is an example. Before becoming a swami, Rama Tirtha was a professor of mathematics, but when he reached the point at which the world became too little for him he began studying, contemplating, and seeking out teachers. Nothing gave him any solace. His spiritual yearning became so intense that he lost his appetite and his ability to sleep. Finally one day he left for the Himalayas in search of Truth. Within two years he returned to the world as an enlightened sage.

A clear understanding of the truth described in the scriptures, a firm belief in it, and the act of reshaping our entire mental landscape in accordance with that knowledge invites the divine grace. Ramana Maharshi, a saint who lived in the first part of the twentieth century, focused his mind one-pointedly on the question "Who am I?" As a result of his constant self-inquiry, spiritual wisdom unfolded, granting him the knowledge "I am That." His mind was so deeply occupied with this awareness that he had no time for any thoughts to the contrary, and this one-pointedness led him to receive the divine grace and to retain it so completely that peace and tranquility emanated from him. People received answers to their questions as they sat quietly in his presence. Similarly intense *vairagya* (non-attachment) and intense *tapas* (austerities) also open a channel through which shaktipata may descend.

In exceptional cases grace may descend suddenly and we undergo an instant transformation for no discernible reason. According to yogic scriptures this may happen to the aspirants known as *bhava pratyaya* yogis—those who had completed a substantial portion of their spiritual journey in their last life but did not quite reach the final destination before the body dropped away.

These *bhava pratyaya* yogis are usually born into an environment that contains all the resources for completing the remaining part of their spiritual journey. Their previous *samskaras* begin to manifest at an early age, making them extraordinary children. The stories of the childhoods of Buddha and Shankaracharya, for example, clearly illustrate the *samskaras* that these saintly souls brought with them from the past.

In other cases, past spiritual characteristics manifest suddenly and an instant transformation occurs. Sri Aurobindo is an example. He was born into an aristocratic Indian family. Educated abroad in the British style, he had little interest in philosophy and spiritual practice. After completing his education, he went to Calcutta to begin a professional career. But destiny had an entirely different plan for him. A powerful thought poured into his mind and he was lost in it. He emerged from that deep and involuntary contemplation a philosopher. Instead of settling in Calcutta, he turned his energy to spiritual pursuits. Eventually he established an ashram in Pondicherry, where he spent the rest of his life. Mahatma Gandhi is another well-known example of such instant transformation.

Bhava pratyaya yogis are like travelers walking toward their destination. When they stop to rest under a fruit tree they yawn, and a luscious fruit drops into their mouth. This doesn't happen to all travelers who stretch out to rest under a tree, only to those with good karmas.

How to Retain the Fruits of Shaktipata

History holds many examples both of the gradual unfoldment of divine grace and of the sudden and complete revelation of the highest truth. One example of the latter is what
happened to the hate-filled Saul, who was struck blind by the
light of heaven on the road to Damascus, and immediately
became Paul. The notorious robber Valmiki was so transformed by the presence of Narada that he was able to receive
the tutelage of the *sapta rishis* (seven sages) and eventually
gain the highest knowledge of Brahman, thus becoming a
brahma rishi. Another notorious cutthroat, Anguli Mala, was
transformed into Ananda by the sight of Buddha.

Endless arguments can be made about whether or not such
incidents are accidental or are the product of good karma,
intense practice, prayer, or deep meditation. Whatever the
cause, it is clear that after they received the grace of God,
these blessed ones invested their time and energy in keeping
the company of wise people, doing their practices, and maintaining an attitude of non-attachment toward the charms and
temptations of the world. This is a clear indication that we too
must commit ourselves to the two pillars of spirituality: practice *(abhyasa)* and non-attachment *(vairagya)*. These are the
means of digesting, assimilating, and retaining the spiritual joy
and illumination of divine grace. We may not understand at a
conscious level how a sincere commitment to practice and
non-attachment becomes the major force behind the assimilation and retention of grace, just as we may not know exactly

how our food is digested and the nutrients assimilated.

Most of those who receive shaktipata are committed to their practice prior to the event, and afterwards they usually engage in their practice with renewed sincerity and force. The problem lies with non-attachment. We often fail to incorporate this principle into our spiritual life, and as a result, even when the grace of God showers upon us, its effect either drains away or is diluted by fear, anxiety, and attachment to worldly obligations. The experience of one of my guru-brothers is a case in point.

In the summer of 1983, Sri Swami Rama was busy transforming the land around his cottage into a garden. One day, when scores of residents were working alongside him in the rain, picking up rocks, digging roots, moving boulders, spreading sod, and planting trees, my guru-brother asked him, "How do you maintain the state of *turiya* (the transcendental state) in the midst of all these activities?"

Swamiji said, "Why not?"

"Only after sitting with my head, neck, and trunk still and straight for an hour or two do I experience even a thousandth of the joy that you gave me during initiation," my brother replied. "How can you possibly stay in that state while you are so active in the external world?"

"How long did you stay in that state when you were initiated?" Swamiji asked.

"Not very long."

"That is why you do not have easy and effortless access to that inner joy which still lies within you," Swamiji replied. "I was in that state for eleven months. My master took care of me."

Later I asked my brother, "Did you come out of that state because you did not want to stay in it, or was there something that prevented you from staying there longer?"

He replied, "It began with a very simple memory of myself as an individual being. Then came a fear of losing myself in that universal unitary blissful awareness. As Swamiji had instructed me to do during such moments, I looked at a ring he had given me. My fear vanished and again I found myself experiencing boundless bliss. This happened several times. Then I started remembering more specifics of myself: I'm married, I have a wife and children, I teach at the university. And suddenly, a thought came, 'If I stay in this state forever, how will I teach my students? Who will support my family?' As these thoughts became clearer and stronger, the intensity of the inner joy became weaker. A couple of hours later the actual experience of the divine bliss was almost gone. Only the alluring memory remained."

As this experience illustrates, the wealth that the master bestows through shaktipata can be retained only if it rests on the firm ground of *vairagya* (non-attachment). Without *vairagya* we cannot assimilate the grace. We are like barren rock—no matter how much it rains, the water runs off.

Non-attachment has nothing to do with abandoning the world and our worldly duties. It is a matter of transforming our attitude toward the world. The essence of non-attachment is knowing that because everything in this world is short-lived, and the goal of life is to attain immortal bliss, we should not place much value on loss and gain, success and failure, honor and insult in our day-to-day existence. This knowledge keeps our mind pure and unaffected amid the turmoil that always accompanies the stream of life. Embracing the principle of non-attachment gives us time and energy for our spiritual pursuits. Those who have cultivated non-attachment can easily commit themselves to self-discipline and self-training, while those who have not are easily distracted and keep straying from the path of self-discipline.

Self-observation and self-analysis are required, however, to help us avoid using the principle of non-attachment to escape from our duties. It is not uncommon for someone who is emotionally disturbed and disappointed by some frustration or failure in his worldly endeavors to think of retiring from the world. This is running away. Only ruthless self-analysis will keep us from confusing running away with non-attachment.

Methodical practice and non-attachment are the two wings of spirituality. If either wing is weak, we cannot soar. By gathering knowledge, keeping the right company, studying genuine scriptures, and most importantly, by being honest with ourselves, we enable both wings to grow in a balanced manner. This much is in our hands. Shaktipata is in the hands of God, which are always open and extended toward us.

A P P E N D I X   A

PREPARATION FOR MANTRA INITIATION

When the body is weak, undernourished, and wracked by stress and when the mind is scattered and confused, it is impossible to concentrate the mind. Good health is the ground on which the practice of mantra meditation blossoms. We prepare the ground by adopting a balanced program to nourish and energize the body, to strengthen the nervous system, and to develop the habit of inner focus that will bring harmony to our scattered mind.

The pages that follow offer a practical, systematic method of working with the body, breath, and mind to develop and maintain good health. You'll find tips on diet and exercise, a program of simple restorative asanas, and detailed instructions on breathing practices and relaxation exercises. These techniques have been simplified and streamlined so that they can be easily practiced by people with hectic schedules. After several months on this program, your body and mind more easily adopt the state of relaxed attention that is the key to a fruitful meditation practice.

A HEALTHY DIET: THE FOUNDATION OF HEALTH

Food is the foundation of health. It can weaken the body, or it can build it up. Specifically, food that is whole and fresh—like fresh fruits, vegetables, and grains—have a marked strengthening effect, for they contain a balanced mix of protein, fat, and carbohydrate—the three basic necessities of the body. In whole, fresh food nature has provided a near-perfect ratio of these nutrients: an abundance of carbohydrate (i.e. starches) for fuel, a moderate amount of protein for rebuilding, and a small amount of fat for lubrication. These foods also contain a wide variety of vitamins and trace minerals that no processed food has, even ones that are "vitamin fortified," for in the refining process much of the vitamin and mineral content is lost.

Fresh foods have vitality. A teacher of mine once told me, "If you eat to live, it is important that the food you eat have life." That "life" is evident when you consider that the grains and beans you eat could just as easily have been sprouted to create new plants. Or you can watch fresh vegetables (that have wilted a bit) perk up with a little water. These foods have life in them, and they give that life to you when you conscientiously consume them.

On the other hand, food can be poison. Foods full of chemical additives and preservatives are a toxic load on your liver. Foods that are not fresh still give you calories and some vitamins (so they do have some value), but they do not give you the complete nourishment your body requires. White sugar, fast food, soda pop, and caffeine give your body some calories (or in the case of caffeine, some artificial energy) but they don't nourish. They leave your body depleted, and craving more nourishment—and there are many in this country who are both overweight and undernourished. Because essential vitamins and minerals are missing in their diets, they do not feel satisfied, and so they overeat.

At the most basic level, food is medicine. It is nourishing and revitalizing when it is fresh, and whole, and fully enjoyed. If eating this way is a big change for you, start with small things: eat a fresh piece of fruit every day, choose a Chinese or Thai restaurant instead of a fast-food place for lunch, or learn a new vegetarian recipe once a week. Make these changes fit into your lifestyle; do them slowly and gently. When you make these changes into habits, you will notice the difference in the flexibility of your body and the clarity of your mind.

EXERCISES FOR OPTIMAL PHYSICAL HEALTH

According to yoga science, the best kind of exercise stimulates the whole body rather than just one muscle group. Yoga postures stretch and stimulate the muscles, ligaments, and joints, restoring elasticity and tone to the body. They promote good circulation and revitalize the internal organs, brain, and nervous system. They enable the respiratory system to perform more efficiently, taking in greater amounts of oxygen and eliminating more toxins, and one of the reasons these exercises are so effective is that the breath is coordinated with the movement. Yoga postures also increase resistance to fatigue and relieve tension. A session of yogic exercises is designed so that exertion is balanced by rest and relaxation.

Yoga postures are not comparable to aerobic exercise, for even during peak performance they do not tax the lungs and heart, and they are not exhausting. Instead, they leave the body revitalized. Yogic postures can be practiced by the strong and the weak, the healthy and the relatively unhealthy. Practicing them will make the body strong and the mind peaceful.

When practicing yoga postures, keep these four key points in mind:

1. Coordinate the breath and movement. Pay attention to your breath; make sure that your movement does not interfere with your breathing pattern, nor vice versa.

2. Stay within your capacity. Be aware of your current level of strength, flexibility, and stamina. Do not force your body into a pose. Stop before you feel fatigued. The object is to feel good when you exercise and after you are finished.

3. Balance the postures. The exertion on a particular limb, organ, or muscle group created by an exercise should be counterbalanced by another exercise. For example, the plow posture stretches the back of the neck and should be followed by the fish posture, which stretches the front of the neck.

4. Relax. Begin and end each exercise session with a systematic relaxation.

How Much to Exercise and When

Yoga postures work with the entire body, especially the internal organs. The effects are subtle, so be careful not to do too much. It is best to start with twenty to thirty minutes of simple postures, and watch how your body responds as you include more advanced exercises in your routine. Your body and your sense of enjoyment are your best guides. Maintaining a regular, moderate practice and following it with a period of relaxation will enable you to expand your capacity in a delightful and amazing way.

Traditionally, morning is thought to be the best time to do postures because the stomach is empty, the colon is clean, and the atmosphere is calm and soothing. However, in the modern world evening may be better because in the morning many people are too busy to have a relaxed session—and even if they have time, stress and lack of proper rest may make them too stiff to exercise comfortably. The best time for an evening practice is before dinner. The main drawback to this, however, is that people are tired or hungry at this time of day (or too full because they couldn't wait to eat, so they stopped off at the local carry-out on the way home). Yoga postures can be done only when the stomach is empty—at least an hour and a half after all but the lightest meals. So if you do choose to practice in the evening, the best option is to make time for yourself by cutting down on evening commitments. Be sure to do a relaxation exercise to eliminate tension and fatigue before you start.

AN ASANA ROUTINE FOR PEOPLE WITH HECTIC SCHEDULES

Exercising doesn't need to be time-consuming. Here is a quick but thorough routine. The whole practice can be done in twenty to thirty minutes. It can be shortened by doing fewer repetitions of the sun salutation or lengthened by doing more. Follow this session with breathing exercises, a systematic relaxation, and meditation.

Stretch!

Begin standing evenly on both feet, with the feet parallel to each other. Lift the pelvis and lengthen the spine as you press down through the feet, lift up through the top of the head, and

press the shoulders down away from your ears. The heart opens, the breath deepens.

Lengthen the arms down, and stretch them out as you slowly lift them out to the side to shoulder height. Pull the fingers toward the body, press the palms away from the body, and keep the shoulders down and relaxed, the heart open, the breath full and deep. Rotate the hands around the wrists in both directions.

Inhale and lift the arms overhead and reach for the sky through the top of the head and the fingertips. Keep the upper back broad and the

ears up out of the shoulders. Press down through the feet, and lengthen the entire spine. Slowly lower the arms with an exhalation.

Arm Swings

Lift both arms up and back on the inhalation, circling them down and forward as you exhale. Continue with deep breathing. Then reverse the direction: circle the arms down and forward as you exhale, and up and back as you inhale.

Side Bends

Stand with the feet hip-width apart. Inhale
and lift the right arm as in a horizontal stretch,
then continue lifting overhead until the upper
arm presses against the ear. Exhale and bend
from the waist to the side directly out over the
left leg. Lengthen both sides of the torso, and
don't allow the torso to roll forward or back.
Keep the right foot pressed into the floor.
Lengthen from the outer right ankle through
the right fingertips. Inhale and lift the right
arm as you straighten back to center. Exhale
the arm down to the side. Repeat on the left side.

Sun Salutation

Stand with the feet parallel to each other and your weight distributed evenly on both feet. Lift the pelvis and lengthen the
spine as you press down through the feet, lift up through the top
of the head, and press the shoulders down away from your ears.
Press the hands together at the center of the chest. The heart
opens, the breath deepens.

Inhale and reach out, up, and back through the arms, lifting
the center of the chest, and looking up. Keep the legs and lower
back straight.

Exhale and keep the head between the arms, and the spine
straight, as you bend forward from the hips. Bend the knees
slightly if the lower back feels strained. Place the palms on the
floor in line with the feet. Relax the head and neck and open the
back of the legs.

SUN SALUTATION

One

Two

Three

Six

Eight

Nine

Four

Five

Seven

Ten

Eleven

Twelve

Inhale and step the right leg back as you bend the left knee and lower the pelvis between the legs. Rest the top of the right foot and leg on the floor. Keep the left knee directly over the left foot, and the hands on the floor in line with the left foot. Arch the back and stretch the head up away from the shoulders as you press the hands into the floor.

As you exhale, step the right foot back to meet the left, toes curled under. Keep the body in a straight line from the top of the head through the heels. The hands are directly under the shoulders.

Lower the knees to the floor, followed by the chest and chin and forehead. Keep the hips lifted, the elbows up, the chest directly between the hands, and the forearms pressed toward the ribs. Then lower the whole torso to the floor as you complete the exhalation.

Inhale and lengthen the head out and up, lifting the chest, shoulders down, elbows in. Reach up through the top of the head, then look up and stretch the front of the neck. Keep the pelvis on the floor and the buttocks firm.

Exhale and lift the hips by straightening the legs, and press the chest toward the thighs. Press the heels toward the floor and broaden the base of the pelvis, allowing the spine to flow toward the floor. Relax the neck and open the shoulders, pressing evenly through the roots of the fingers.

Inhale and bring the right leg forward between the hands in line with the fingers. Lower the top of the left foot and left leg to the floor. Drop the pelvis between the legs. Keep the right knee over the right foot. Stretch up and draw the ears out of the shoulders.

Exhale and lift the pelvis, straightening both legs as you step the left foot up to the right. Keep the hands on the floor in line with the feet. Bend the knees slightly if necessary. Broaden the pelvis, open the back of the legs, drop the head, and relax the neck.

Inhale and reach out and up through the spine, stretching the arms alongside the head, keeping the shoulders down. Keep the spine straight as you lift up and then back, lifting and opening the chest.

Exhale and come to the starting standing position, with the hands together at the center of the chest. Repeat three to six times.

Agni Sara

Stand with the feet hip-width apart, knees slightly bent, and hands on the thighs. Keep the arms straight, and rest the weight of the torso on the thighs. As you begin to exhale, apply the root lock by contracting the anal and urinary sphincter muscles. Holding the root lock, continue exhaling and contract the lower abdominal muscles, and then the upper abdominal muscles, moving the abdominal wall in and up. Complete the exhalation and the contraction at the same time. Hold the breath out, bring the hollow of the neck to the chin, and draw the upper abdomen in and up under the ribs by expanding the chest as if inhaling (*uddiyana bandha*). Lower the abdomen without pause, release the chin, begin inhaling, and

release the upper abdominal muscles. Release the lower abdominal muscles and then the root lock as you continue inhaling. Repeat the whole sequence five to ten times or more, without pausing. The practice should be smooth and slow, without gasping—with a fluid wave-like motion.

If you have high blood pressure, ulcers, a hernia, or heart disease, avoid lifting the abdomen, and instead simply contract all the abdominal muscles on the exhalation and smoothly release on the inhalation.

Agni sara is contraindicated during pregnancy and menstruation.

Spinal Twist

Sit with the spine straight and the legs extended out in front. Bend the right knee and place the foot on the floor outside the left knee. Inhale and straighten the spine by drawing the abdomen toward the right thigh with the left arm. Exhale and begin twisting to the right from the lower abdomen. Place the right hand on the floor near the back right hip. If possible, put the left arm over the outside of the right leg and grasp the right foot or either leg with the left hand. Look over the right shoulder.

Continue straightening the spine as you inhale, and twisting as you exhale. Repeat on the other side.

Bridge Pose

Lie on the back with the knees bent and the feet on the floor near the pelvis, hip-width apart. The arms are alongside the body, palms down. Exhale and press the lower back into the floor and lift the tailbone. Continue exhaling and roll up the spine, lifting the pelvis, navel center, and chest. Roll the shoulders under and down as you broaden the upper back and press the sternum toward the chin. Keep the pelvis lifted, and hold and breathe. Grasp the ankles with the hands if possible, and press the torso up. Roll down slowly from the top of the spine to the tailbone.

Finish with a relaxation in the corpse pose.

BREATHING EXERCISES

About Breath and the Pranic Force

The scriptures say that "breath is life and life is breath." Breath is the link between the individual and the cosmic being, and between the body and mind. A healthy breathing pattern ensures the health of both body and mind.

The yogic breathing techniques are called *pranayama,* which literally means expanding the vital force, or gaining control over the activities of the vital force within. The following five techniques provide a systematic method of preparing for classical yogic breathing practices: sandbag breathing, deep breathing, diaphragmatic breathing, alternate nostril breathing, and 2:1 breathing. The first three exercises build on each other, strengthening awareness and the capacity to breathe diaphragmatically. Once diaphragmatic breathing is established, alternate nostril breathing, 2:1 breathing, and other pranayamas can be introduced.

Sandbag Breathing

This practice will strengthen the abdominal and diaphragmatic muscles. It will also help regulate the motion of the lungs in concert with the movement of the muscles of the diaphragm.

To begin, you'll need a five-pound sandbag packed tight enough to retain its shape, but not so tight that it is rock-hard. You may use another kind of weight, but make sure it is soft and is comfortable when placed on the abdomen.

Begin by lying on your back and relaxing your body from head to toe. Calm your breath. Now gently place the sandbag on your abdomen. If you have heart problems, lung problems, or blood pressure abnormalities, place the sandbag on the muscles below the navel, but make sure that no part of the sandbag is supported by the pelvic girdle.

Close your eyes and breathe. Feel how the sandbag rises as you inhale and drops as you exhale. You must make an effort to inhale, but the exhalation should be effortless. After three to five minutes, remove the sandbag and relax on your back for a few more minutes.

If you practice regularly, you may want to increase the weight of the sandbag every two weeks. Do this gradually, staying within your comfort range, but do not exceed fifteen pounds.

Deep Breathing

Breathing deeply allows you to experience the full capacity of your lungs. It brings more oxygen to your tissues, and rids you of wastes. It also loosens the muscles of the rib cage, allowing for greater expansion. The net effect is revitalization.

Lie on your back in the corpse pose and take ten deep breaths. Pay special attention to the exhalation, taking care to exhale fully. Do not pause between breaths. Let the breath flow smoothly, silently, and without jerks. Notice how refreshed you feel after completing these ten breaths.

Diaphragmatic Breathing

One of the first aims of yoga is to reestablish good breathing habits as a means of improving both physical and mental health. Restoring the habit of diaphragmatic breathing accomplishes this effectively. Diaphragmatic breathing enables you to feel your best, gain emotional control and balance, and reduce fatigue and stress. The habit of diaphragmatic breathing is basic to all other yogic breathing practices.

The diaphragm divides the torso into two separate chambers: the thorax and the abdomen. The diaphragm forms the floor of the thorax, and rests against the base of the lungs. The diaphragm is a dome-shaped muscle that relaxes during exhalation, pressing against the lungs from below. It contracts on inhalation. In a healthy person the movement of the diaphragm is responsible for seventy-five percent of the exchange of gases

in the lungs. However, the diaphragm is often tense, blocking natural breathing, and causing fatigue, tension, and other more serious problems.

You can learn what correct diaphragmatic breathing feels like by assuming the crocodile posture—lie on your stomach with your legs a comfortable distance apart. The toes can be pointed in or out, whichever is more comfortable. Fold the arms in front of the body, resting the hands on the biceps. Position the arms so that the base of the rib cage touches the floor.

Place the forehead on the forearms. When you inhale in this position, the abdomen expands, pressing against the floor, and the back gently rises. As you exhale the abdomen contracts, and the back gently falls. Both of these effects are produced by the movement of the diaphragm.

Establish the habit of breathing diaphragmatically at all times. You can do this by practicing the crocodile pose three times a day for five to ten minutes. When you're finished, roll onto your back and observe the abdomen as it expands and contracts with the breath. Next, sit in a chair and again watch your breathing, keeping the abdomen relaxed. The last step is to stand as you continue to breathe diaphragmatically. Practice regularly until diaphragmatic breathing becomes a habit.

Alternate Nostril Breathing

Alternate nostril breathing, also known as channel purification or *nadi shodhanam,* is a means of purifying the subtle energy channels in the body and bringing the activities of the nervous system to a state of balance. To do this practice:

1. Sit with the legs crossed in the easy pose, or sit on a chair with the feet flat on the floor. Make sure the head, neck, and trunk are aligned.

2. Bring the right hand to the nose, folding the index finger and the middle finger so that the right thumb can be used to close the right nostril and the ring finger can be used to close the left nostril.

3. Close the left nostril and exhale completely through the right nostril.

4. At the end of the exhalation, close the right nostril and inhale through the left nostril slowly and completely. The inhalation and exhalation should be of equal duration.

5. Repeat this cycle of exhalation through the right nostril and inhalation through the left nostril two more times.

6. At the end of the third inhalation, keep the right nostril closed and exhale completely through the left nostril.

7. At the end of the exhalation, close the left nostril and inhale through the right nostril.

8. Repeat two more times, exhaling through the left nostril and inhaling through the right nostril.

The pattern looks like this:

EXHALE	INHALE
Right	Left
Right	Left
Right	Left
Left	Right
Left	Right
Left	Right

This cycle can be repeated as many times as you wish. Make sure you do an equal number of inhalations and exhalations through each nostril. With practice you will gradually be able to lengthen the duration of the inhalation and exhalation.

2:1 Breathing

This breathing practice is essential for people who live where the air is polluted, because it cleans the lungs and purifies the blood. You may do it either in the corpse pose or in a sitting posture. The method is as follows:

1. First establish a pattern of breathing so that the inhalation and exhalation are of equal duration. You can count to make sure that the length of your inhalation and exhalation are equal.

2. After you have established a pattern of even breathing (it may take a few days or even a couple of weeks), resolve to exhale longer than you inhale. For example, count to ten while inhaling, and to fifteen while exhaling. As your practice continues, add a few more counts periodically, and see how comfort-

able you feel. Set a goal for yourself so that within two or three months you are inhaling to a count of ten, and exhaling to a count of twenty. When you have accomplished this, maintain it for a while.

3. After a few more months, continue to lengthen your breath, always keeping the exhalation twice as long as the inhalation (e.g. if you inhale in twelve counts, exhale in twenty-four counts; if you inhale in fifteen counts, exhale in thirty counts).

The following checklist will help you to evaluate your breathing:

1. The breath flows smoothly.
2. There is no pause between breaths.
3. The breath flows silently.
4. Exhalation and inhalation are of approximately equal duration (except for 2:1 breathing).
5. The breath is deep, yet there is little movement of the upper chest.

In summary, the goal is to breathe deeply with no jerks, no pause, and no noise.

RELAXATION TECHNIQUES

Relaxation is important for resting the body, for often sleep does not give rest. The relaxation techniques described here are designed to relieve the body of tension that interferes with blood flow, energy flow, and rejuvenation. Daily practice of relaxation techniques allows the body to repair itself, creating sustained energy and greater health.

Relaxation in the Crocodile Pose

Lie on the stomach, placing the legs a comfortable distance apart and pointing the toes in or out, whichever is more comfortable. Fold the arms in front of the body, resting the hands on the biceps. Position the arms so that the chest does not touch the floor. Then place the forehead on the forearms and breathe diaphragmatically. You may use a cloth beneath the nostrils to keep from inhaling dust. Observe the breath and let it become deep and smooth. While inhaling, feel the abdominal muscles gently press against the floor; while exhaling, feel the abdomen contract. Let the body relax completely.

Relaxation in the Corpse Pose

The word *relaxation* may be somewhat misleading. If you "try" to relax, the effort is bound to fail. Relaxation must be learned systematically and then allowed to progress naturally. In relaxation, one learns the art of letting go.

There are many methods of yoga relaxation. The following exercise forms the base from which many other exercises may be learned. It is effective in relieving tension, and it helps to bring the mind into a state of relaxed concentration.

Lie on your back. Use a thin cushion under the head. Cover your body with a sheet or thin shawl. Place the legs a comfortable distance apart. The arms are slightly separated from the body, and the palms are turned up. Most importantly, the spine should not be bent to either side. Take time to adjust your posture, and then become still.

Close your eyes, and be aware of the presence of your body, the space around you, and the place on which your body rests.

RELAXATION SEQUENCE

forehead
eyebrows and eyes
nose *pause for two relaxed breaths*
cheeks
mouth
jaw
chin
neck
shoulders
upperarms
lower arms
hands
fingers
fingertips *pause for two relaxed breaths*

fingers
hands
lower arms
upper arms
shoulders
chest
heart center *pause for two relaxed breaths*
stomach
naval region
pelvic region
upper legs
lower legs
feet
toes *pause for four relaxed breaths*

Figure 1

Observe your entire body from head to toe. Cultivate and enjoy the perfect stillness of your body.

Be aware of the slow and gentle movement of your breath. Observe each exhalation and inhalation, and let the breath become deep and diaphragmatic. Breathing out, release all tension, waste, fatigue, and worry. Inhale energy, strength, tranquility, and a sense of well-being. Do not pause between breaths.

Next, survey your body mentally. You will naturally release tension in the places where you observe it. This process of letting go of tension is the relaxation process. Proceed from the head to the toes, and then back to the head, following the sequence set out in Figure 1 on page 213.

Now reverse the order and proceed upward, this time without any pauses.

Some practice will be required to complete this exercise without a lapse of attention. If your mind wanders, gently bring it back to the relaxation process.

After progressing through the whole body, gently relax your mind. Turn your attention to the quiet flow of your breath, and observe the entire breathing process. Rest for a few minutes and feel that this subtle stream of breath is a link joining you to the cosmos. Experience the harmony and peace. Then roll onto your side and sit up.

31-Point Relaxation

In this exercise the mind is focused in sequence on specific nerve-rich points of the upper body. Physically, this exercise causes a complete release of muscular tension, and a balancing

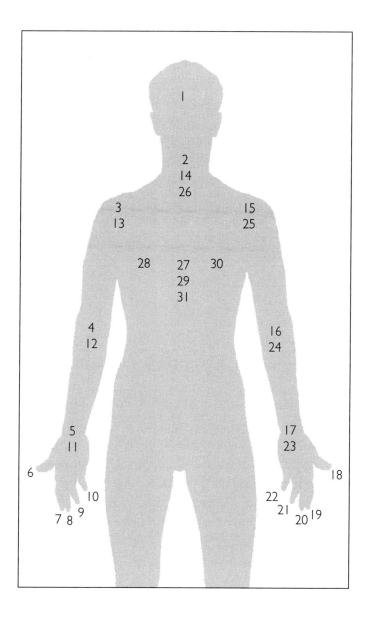

Figure 2

of subtle energies. Mentally, it trains the mind to be one-pointed and inward, leading one toward greater self-awareness.

To begin this practice, first do a systematic relaxation. When you are centered and relaxed, bring your attention to the point between the eyebrows, and mentally repeat the number "1." Keep the attention fixed at that point for one or two seconds. In the same manner, concentrate on each of the numbered points in succession, as pictured in Figure 2 on page 215.

If you are having trouble keeping your mind focused, move from point to point more quickly, or admit that you are too tired to do this exercise now, and resolve to try again when you are more rested. It is important to stop if you are sleepy or if your mind is wandering—if you continue, you aren't practicing concentrating your mind, you are only practicing sleeping.

Repeating the exercise from points 1 to 31 a second time increases your mental endurance. Practice daily for two weeks or longer, doing two 31-point exercises in succession until you can easily travel through all the points with full attention day after day.

Meditation: The Next Step

Once you have adopted a healthy diet, have restored some flexibility to your body by practicing a simple set of asanas, have begun to develop the habit of breathing deeply and smoothly from the diaphragm, and have gained some proficiency in simple, systematic relaxation techniques, you are ready to begin working directly with the mind in meditation. Chapter 4 gives detailed instructions for establishing a meditation practice based on the natural sound of the breath.

A P P E N D I X   B

How to Do a *Purash Charana*

To take full advantage of mantra initiation it is important to undertake a systematic practice traditionally known as *purash charana,* which literally means "first step on the path of spirituality" (*purash* means "in front of; first" and *charana* means "foot or step"). This practice consists of five main components: *japa,* repetition of mantra; *homa,* making an offering to fire; *tarpana,* watering (or nourishing) the body and mind with water sanctified by the power of mantra; *marjana,* cleansing the body and mind with the water sanctified with the power of mantra; and *sadhaka seva,* serving adepts and aspirants on the path.

JAPA

Japa is the repetition of a mantra. It can be vocalized, or repeated silently, or be purely mental. The latter two are considered superior to the first, as they require greater concentration. Concentration requires attention. We pay attention only when we are interested; interest comes from feeling, and feeling develops when there is a loving relationship between the mantra and ourselves. Because mantra is made of sound, developing this loving relationship can be difficult. But if we could somehow understand that it is God, in the form of mantra, that has entered our mind and heart, we would have great respect and love for it.

Sometimes, despite our knowledge of mantric metaphysics, we still fail to comprehend that God, or the Divine Being, can be with us in the form of sound. Mind has great difficulty comprehending the Absolute Reality if it does not have a name or form. That is why sages have given us equivalents to mantras in the form of yantras or deities. As we have seen in chapter 7, there is perfect correspondence among mantra, yantra, mandala, and deity. However, yogis prefer not to introduce mantra in its anthropomorphic form because this concept often creates a conflict in the minds of students who do not understand the underlying metaphysics. Although a personified form of God (which corresponds to a particular mantra) can help to establish a relationship with the divine force, this is not helpful unless the symbols behind the mythology are properly understood.

In our scientific era it is easy to accept the idea that sound and light are interchangeable. The technology of fax machines, for example, clearly demonstrates how sound, light, and images can be transformed into one another. The same is true of mantra. The yantra or the deity is simply the pictorial manifestation of mantra. To practice a mantra, it is not necessary to know the exact yantra or personified form of deity corresponding to it. However, a general knowledge of all these components and the ability to incorporate them into our *sadhana* can help us gain spiritual experience faster and easier.

If the concept of yantra and deity conflicts with your religious upbringing, simply focus your practice on the mantra itself. But if you have a good grasp of mantric cosmology and metaphysics, and have thereby transcended their cultish aspects, then ask your teacher about the yantra that accompanies your mantra practice.

While you are doing your daily practice of mantra meditation, and before you embark on a purash charana, explore ways of establishing a personal relationship with the impersonal aspect of God. Keep reinforcing the idea that mantra is not simply a sound or a prayer, but an embodiment of the Divine Being. The more this idea seeps into your heart, the more clearly the concept of *ishta deva,* the form of formless God, will emerge in your consciousness. Once this concept is clear, it will become easy for your psyche to communicate blissfully with your own higher self, which is an integral part of the universal consciousness. The emergence of the *ishta deva* fills your heart with love and devotion, and consequently your mind loses interest in wandering from one object to another. At this stage the mantra begins to flow effortlessly and spontaneously. This is important, for without true love and devotion for the mantra, the mind finds very little joy in mantra japa, and you will have to force it to be aware of the mantra. This means that your mind will be engaged with the verbal form of the mantra.

When you are ready to undertake methodical practice of purash charana, make a resolution to complete a specific number of mantra repetitions within a certain time. The number of repetitions a day, and the number of days required to complete a purash charana, differs for each mantra. At first it is better to take the smallest course, so you can complete it without a major struggle. One round of japa consists of 100 repetitions of the mantra. For example, if your mantra has five syllables, then you may complete 500,000 repetitions by repeating 25 rounds per day for 200 days. But if your mantra consists of 24 syllables, it is better to do only 10 rounds a day and complete 125,000 repetitions in 125 days. Later, as time and energy permit, you can undertake a bigger course of purash charana. The scriptures give general guidelines for defining the course of purash charana, but the specifics can be supplied only by a teacher who has gone through the practices and experienced its subtleties firsthand.

HOMA

Homa entails making offerings into the fire while repeating the mantra one-tenth the number of times you repeated it during the japa portion of the practice. For example, if you repeated the mantra 500,000 times while doing japa, you repeat it again with the fire offering 50,000 times. The items offered into the fire differ from tradition to tradition, and from mantra to mantra, but they usually include herbs, grains, and ghee.

Knowing how to make a fireplace and what kind of fuel to use requires guidance from teachers and the scriptures. In fact, *homa* as well as the next two components of purash charana— *tarpana* and *marjana*—must be practiced with the assistance of a teacher or some other experienced person unless the student is an expert in the technicalities these practices involve. Every act in the process of *homa*—gathering the sticks, arranging them in the fireplace, igniting the fire, invoking the divine force that resides in the fire element, and putting the offerings in their proper place—should be done with precision and accuracy. It is important to remember that when *homa* is a component of purash charana it is not a fire ceremony in the religious sense. Rather, *homa* is a way of invoking, receiving, and honoring the divinity that pervades the internal and external world. Japa, the first component of purash charana, awakens the power of mantra within our psyche; *homa*, the second component, awakens the power of mantra in the external world. The mantric forces within and without now begin to converge, for the *homa* helps us to realize that the mantric force pervades the realm outside as well as inside us. It is a way of dismantling the wall between microcosm and macrocosm, the inner and the external realms.

TARPANA

Tarpana means "watering, refreshing, nourishing, or invigorating." As in *homa*, a teacher or a senior practitioner of mantra usually assists by sanctifying the water, which symbolizes the sap of life, by performing *mudras* (gestures) and reciting mantras. As the practitioner, you concentrate at the heart center, invoking the presence of the Divine, and sprinkling water on yourself while repeating the mantra you have been using for the purash charana one-tenth as many times as you repeated it during the *homa*. In our example, you would repeat the mantra 5,000 times. By engaging in intense concentration and visualization, you feel as though you are transformed into the deity or yantric form of mantra, and you propitiate the divine force with an offering of water.

Marjana

Marjana, the fourth component of purash charana, means "cleansing or washing." Here, you fill a vessel with water, invite the mantra and its corresponding deity to reside in the vessel, and then sprinkle the water on your own body while repeating the mantra one-tenth as many times as in *tarpana,* or five hundred times in our example.

Sadhaka Seva

Sadhaka seva means "serving other *sadhakas* (seekers), and adepts." To perform it you serve one-tenth the number of people as the number of mantras you repeated in *marjana.* In our example, you would serve fifty aspirants. This is done by honoring *sadhakas,* giving them food and clothing, and performing other actions that demonstrate your love and respect. The purpose is to cultivate humility as well as to receive their blessings. This final component of purash charana creates an environment for receiving guidance from learned people.

Obstacles to Completing the Practice

This brief discussion of purash charana is based on general descriptions available in the texts. You must go to the teacher who gave you mantra initiation to receive specific instructions, as these instructions vary with each mantra. Furthermore, you learn the subtle points by observing other *sadhakas* and by offering your assistance when they are undergoing a purash charana.

According to the tradition, it is not easy to complete a purash charana without running into obstacles. In most cases the practice is undertaken, dropped, renewed, and completed only after repeated attempts. Internal enemies—the obstacles hidden deep in the unconscious mind—become agitated and aggressive as an unlit corner of the mind is about to be illuminated with the brilliance of mantra. Our karmic foes often manifest during the purash charana in the form of disease, procrastination, negligence, doubt, sloth, grief, anger, desire, hatred, jealousy, greed, and so on. And as these obstacles emerge, we become disheartened, often blaming the practice itself as the cause of these obstacles.

The higher the goal, the more hurdles have to be crossed. In the case of meditative and contemplative mantras, the size and number of obstacles arising during the purash charana is relatively small. But during the practice of the *maha* mantras described in chapter 6, the obstacles can be numerous and formidable. Because the purpose of a purash charana of a *maha* mantra is to annihilate ignorance (the ultimate cause of our bondage), the obstacles arising can be subtle and quite potent. Therefore the sages advise us to practice complementary mantras, whose direct purpose is to eliminate obstacles and their causes so that we may continue our spiritual journey without struggling.

THE *GAYATRI* AND *MAHA MRTYUNJAYA* MANTRAS

Traditionally the *gayatri* and *maha mrtyunjaya* mantras are given for the purpose of eliminating obstacles. In fact, in the ancient Vedic tradition, one of these mantras was given to prospective students when they were still children, long before they knew anything about spirituality. These mantras were an inseparable part of the child's spiritual education. As a result, such children grew as radiant spiritual seekers, and when they embarked on their spiritual quest during their youth, they had very few obstacles to overcome.

The *gayatri* mantra is traditionally called "the Mother of the Vedas." Its practice enabled the sages to receive revelation of all other mantras, for this mantra shuts down mental noise, washes off karmic impurities, purifies the ego, sharpens the intellect, and illuminates the inner being with the light which flows directly from the Source. The *gayatri* mantra connects us to the teacher within, helping us receive inner guidance and inner inspiration. The process of purification begins in the deep unconscious and gradually pervades all aspects of our personality. We become new and fully transformed, from inside out. Although the transformation is rarely instantaneous, the effect of this mantra is immense and everlasting.

The *maha mrtyunjaya* mantra, on the other hand, is a healing and nourishing mantra. In a sense, it is the heart of the Vedas. The healing force awakened by this mantra sends forth its ripples from body to psyche and from psyche to soul. It strengthens our powers of will, knowledge, and action, and it unleashes enthusiasm, courage, and determination. The vibration of this mantra awakens the internal healing force while attracting nature's healing agents, creating an environment in which both forces converge. The *maha mrtyunjaya* mantra connects us to the healer within, and it helps us to receive full nourishment from food, herbs, or any discipline undertaken for our total well-being.

According to the sages, there are two ways of overcoming obstacles to our spiritual unfoldment: either clear away the hurdles by overcoming our weaknesses, consequently gaining inner strength; or strengthen the strong part of ourselves even further, freeing ourselves from weakness. *Gayatri* practice reinforces the first method, and *maha mrtyunjaya* the second. *Gayatri* focuses on cleansing, *maha mrtyunjaya* on healing. Ultimately, both practices lead to the same goal.

Gayatri practice is suitable for those who may be struggling with confusion, doubt, skepticism, lack of self-trust, and lack of direction. It is good for those who are tired of trying this and trying that and for those who want to get in touch with their own intuition rather than leaning on friends, teachers, books, tapes, and other external aids.

The *maha mrtyunjaya* practice, on the other hand, is suitable for those who are struggling with lack of energy, a sense of hopelessness, grief, and illness, as well as lack of enthusiasm, courage, and determination. It is good for those who want to get in touch with their own healing force. This mantra is especially good for those in the health professions because it helps prevent burn-out by continually replacing the energy that healers channel to patients.

Pandit Rajmani Tigunait, Ph.D., is the Spiritual Head of the Himalayan Institute, a life-long practitioner of meditation, and a scholar of the ancient scriptures. He is a disciple of Sri Swami Rama of the Himalayas, and has studied with various adepts and scholars in the ancient guru/disciple lineage. He is a regular contributor to *Yoga International* magazine and is the author of the books *Seven Systems of Indian Philosophy, Yoga on War and Peace, The Tradition of the Himalayan Masters, Shakti Sadhana,* and *Inner Quest.* He gives lectures and seminars throughout the United States and abroad.

THE HIMALAYAN INSTITUTE

Founded in 1971 by Swami Rama, the Himalayan Institute has been dedicated to helping people grow physically, mentally, and spiritually by combining the best knowledge of both the East and the West.

Our international headquarters is located on a beautiful 400-acre campus in the rolling hills of the Pocono Mountains of northeastern Pennsylvania. The atmosphere here is one to foster growth, increased inner awareness, and calm. Our grounds provide a wonderfully peaceful and healthy setting for our seminars and extended programs. Students from around the world join us here to attend programs in such diverse areas as hatha yoga, meditation, stress reduction, Ayurveda, nutrition, Eastern philosophy, psychology, and other subjects. Whether the programs are for weekend meditation retreats, week-long seminars on spirituality, months-long residential programs, or holistic health services, the attempt here is to provide an environment of gentle

inner progress. We invite you to join with us in the ongoing process of personal growth and development.

The Institute is a nonprofit organization. Your membership in the Institute helps to support its programs. Please call or write for information on becoming a member.

INSTITUTE PROGRAMS, SERVICES, AND FACILITIES

Institute programs share an emphasis on conscious holistic living and personal self-development, including:

Special weekend or extended seminars to teach skills and techniques for increasing your ability to be healthy and enjoy life

Meditation retreats and advanced meditation and philosophical instruction

Vegetarian cooking and nutritional training

Hatha yoga and exercise workshops

Residential programs for self-development

Holistic health services and Ayurvedic Rejunenation Programs through the Institute's Center for Health and Healing.

A Quarterly Guide to Programs and Other Offerings is free within the USA. To request a copy, or for further information, call 800-822-4547 or 570-253-5551, fax 570-253-9078, email bqinfor@himalayaninstitute.org, write the Himalayan Institute, RR 1, Box 400, Honesdale, PA 18431-9706 USA, or visit our website at www.himalayaninstitute.org.

THE HIMALAYAN INSTITUTE PRESS

योगः कर्मसु कौशलम्

The Himalayan Institute Press has long been regarded as "The Resource for Holistic Living." We publish dozens of titles, as well as audio and video tapes, that offer practical methods for living harmoniously and achieving inner balance. Our approach addresses the whole person—body, mind, and spirit—integrating the latest scientific knowledge with ancient healing and self-development techniques.

As such, we offer a wide array of titles on physical and psychological health and well-being, spiritual growth through meditation and other yogic practices, as well as translations of yogic scriptures.

Our sidelines include the Japa Kit for meditation practice, the original Neti™ Pot, the ideal tool for sinus and allergy sufferers, and The Breath Pillow,™ a unique tool for learning health-supportive and diaphragmatic breathing.

Subscriptions are available to a bimonthly magazine, *Yoga International*, which offers thought-provoking articles on all aspects of meditation and yoga, including yoga's sister science, Ayurveda.

For a free catalog call 800-822-4547 or 570-253-5551, email hibooks@himalayaninstitute.org, fax 570-253-6360, write the Himalayan Institute Press, RR 1, Box 405, Honesdale, PA 18431-9709, USA, or visit our website at www.himalayaninstitute.org.